ETHAN ALLEN'S
NEW AMERICAN STYLE

ETHAN ALLEN'S NEW AMERICAN STYLE

STAGE-BY-STAGE DECORATING FOR YOUR HOME

ETHAN ALLEN WITH VIVIA CHEN

CLARKSON POTTER/PUBLISHERS
NEW YORK

Published by Clarkson Potter/Publishers, New York, New York. Member of the Crown Publishing Group.

Random House, Inc. New York, Toronto, London, Sydney, Auckland

www.randomhouse.com

Clarkson N. Potter is a trademark and Potter and colophon are registered trademarks of Random House, Inc.

Printed in China

Design by Kayo Der Sarkissian

Library of Congress Cataloging-in-Publication Data

Ethan Allen's new American style / by Ethan Allen with Vivia Chen.—1st ed.

1. Ethan Allen, Inc. 2. Interior decoration—United States. I. Title: New American style. II. Chen, Vivia. III. Ethan Allen, Inc.

NK2004.3.E87 2001

747—dc21 00-044087

ISBN 0-609-60156-3

10 9 8 7 6 5 4 3 2 1

First Edition

ACKNOWLEDGMENTS

Ethan Allen is very pleased to have this opportunity to bring out a sensible guide to planning and designing beautiful rooms that fit your lifestyle. We hope that this book will become a valuable resource in your decorating library.

Many people have been a part of this process, and we would like to say thank you to everyone involved. To the many individuals at Ethan Allen who contributed to this project, especially the Ethan Allen design department and photo studio, who are responsible for the beautiful room settings you see in this book—thank you. To the freelance photographers and stylists who also contributed their talents to this project—thank you. And to the many homeowners who so graciously allowed us to disrupt their daily lives in order to show you their beautiful homes—thank you. We would also like to thank everyone at Clarkson Potter who guided us through our first venture in book publishing.

At Ethan Allen, we have a true passion for what we do—helping people bring their dreams of beautiful, comfortable homes to life. We hope this book will be a helpful tool as you begin to explore your own personal style and plan the home of your dreams.

CONTENTS

INTRODUCTION

You probably have some vision of your perfect home: a rustic seaside cottage bathed in natural light; a starkly minimalist loft with dramatic ceilings and skyline views; an elegant mansion filled with gilded trimmings. But no matter what your taste, you want your home to be not just beautiful and stylish but also comfortable and practical—it is, after all, where you and your family *live*. So how do you balance style and comfort? How do you achieve your ideal on a sensible budget and within a reasonable time frame? How do you make the hundreds of individual choices—from floor finishes and window treatments to furniture purchases and the placement of accessories—that make up a cohesive decorating statement? These are important questions. This book provides the answers.

BE REALISTIC AND EXPECT EVOLUTION

The first, most important answer—an answer that's relevant to every question is a simple suggestion: be realistic. Be realistic about your budget and your schedule, of course. But also be realistic about your needs, the uses for your rooms, and who is going to be doing what, where, and when. Understand that your house should be more than a decorating statement: it should be a home that serves the needs and desires of many people, including your children as well as your dinner guests and weekend visitors. This realization is the first step toward creating a home that makes your life easier and makes you happier.

The most intimidating aspect of decorating is looking at an empty house and thinking that you have to finish the floors, paint the walls and ceilings, fill it with furniture, hang art, and arrange knickknacks by the time your in-laws arrive for dinner on Friday night. If you approach decorating with such a high-pressure all-at-once deadline, there's a good chance that you'll be paralyzed with fear and indecision—and either make overly hasty decisions or, worse, make none at all.

Instead, realize that your home can—and should—evolve over time, as you and your family evolve. If you plan your investments of effort and money sensibly, this evolution can be painless and natural, and your home can be comfortable and stylish every step of the way.

So, what is sensible planning? First, your decorating scheme should begin with the essentials: figure out what you want your overall look to be, then choose a few elements to lay the foundation for that look. Although it may seem obvious to begin with the basics, it takes discipline to focus your attention on these core decisions and to make the necessary commitments. You may be much more at ease choosing a nightstand or a coffee table than a wall unit or a sofa; smaller purchases are less expensive and seem less permanent. But they don't build the necessary foundation of your design.

Once you've chosen your general style and installed the fundamental building blocks that make your home livable, you can add occasional pieces and accents to fill out the rooms and round out the decor. This evolution may take a few months or a few years or even your entire lifetime—whatever makes you comfortable. But decorating will be enjoyable instead of stressful, and the results will be a true reflection of your tastes.

Once you settle on an overall look, just a few smart choices can send you well on your way to an ideal room: a fresh paint job and a bed are all this room really needs; the chair plus a vase of flowers on a makeshift table produce a more filled-out room.

DEFINE YOUR PRIORITIES AND ASSESS YOUR ASSETS

Before you grab your credit cards and rush out shopping, take a few minutes to figure out your priorities. Think about each room: What will you use it for? What furniture do you need to do those things? Do you already own these pieces? What do you own but want to replace? What do you need to buy for the first time? What style will best serve your needs *and* your aesthetic goals?

Most often, a room's primary use is pretty obvious. Bedroom? Sleeping. Dining room? Eating. But think carefully about other uses. For example, clothing storage is an important priority in many bedrooms; getting dressed, applying makeup, and talking on the telephone are other things that you may do there. And what do you need to accomplish these tasks? A dresser or armoire for storing clothes; customized closets for housing an extensive shoe collection; a full-length mirror for getting dressed; a vanity in a well-lit location for applying makeup; a comfortable chair and a small table for talking on the phone.

If you plan to do all these things in your bedroom, you should prioritize your design decisions to accommodate all of them. So even if you've always dreamed of a four-poster bed, you may be better off finding the perfect wing chair that you'll sit in every night while you chat on the phone. Let your lifestyle dictate your furniture priorities and purchases.

Don't be surprised to find that your most important decisions involve the biggest, most expensive pieces of furniture—for instance, in the living room such big-ticket items as a comfortable sofa will establish the decor of the entire room. So the style of the sofa should be the foundation on which you build the other pieces. If your goal is a sleek, contemporary look, be sure to start with a sleek, contemporary sofa—even if it means a little more shopping.

The secondary goal in this bedroom is a quiet, comfortable place to read—perfectly carved out of this inviting corner.

BEDROOM DECORATING PRIORITIES

HAVE	NEED	WANT
mattress/box spring		
		four-poster frame
bedside table		
dresser		
	armoire	
		vanity
	armchair	
		bedside table
blinds		
		curtains
	paint ceiling	
		paint walls
		paint trim

Getting a good deal on a country-style sofa is not, in fact, getting a good deal; it's wasting time, effort, and money on something that you'll eventually replace because it doesn't fit your look.

To help you define your priorities, create a chart for each room that outlines these goals. The most important aspect of this exercise is figuring out the difference between the things you *need* and the things you *want*. For instance, if your ceiling has cracks, peeling paint, and water stains, you *need* a paint job. On the other hand, if the walls are painted a pristine white, you don't *need* to paint the walls—you *want* to.

Now that you've divided up your needs and desires, you have a pretty clear picture of your priorities: the most important items are those in the *need* column. This is not to say that you should ignore your *want* column; just focus on your needs. You also have an understanding of some of your assets—the things in the *have* column. But take the opportunity to inventory your other important assets: the natural bones of your home. These are the interior details that made you fall in love with your home in the first place: high ceilings, moldings, windows, light, wood floors, fireplaces, built-in bookshelves, French doors, sunken rooms, staircases, wainscoting, closets. Exterior aspects will also factor in: views, landscaping, garden, pool, terrace, porch. Finally, consider your location: the landscaping and architecture of your neighbors' homes, proximity to beach, mountains, lakes, or rivers, the character of your neighborhood.

All of these natural bones should inform your decorating approach and can help you set your priorities. For example, a center-of-town Victorian, an Art Deco apartment-building, an industrial loft, and a shingle-style beach house all have very different needs. Each style boasts distinct assets that you'll want to exploit. At the beach house, you'll want to maintain easy outdoor access and take advantage of the views, light, and breezes; to do this, you may want to leave the windows, floors, and walls fairly bare and concentrate on decorating the deck. In the Victorian, the moldings, fireplaces, and wainscoting may cry out for a richly layered look of overstuffed furniture with a profusion of pillows, rugs, and art. The sunken

living room in the Art Deco apartment seems to require chrome accents, sweeping curves, and vintage advertising posters. And to take advantage of the loft's high ceilings, brick walls, exposed pipes, and fantastic views, you may want to leave the windows bare, hang a single charcoal drawing, and install a modernist sofa.

Don't underestimate these types of assets: appraising them will help you to define your decorating priorities and to choose furniture and wall, window, and floor treatments that reflect your style.

Of course, your home may have some drawbacks that you'll want to camouflage or correct. Have your floors seen better days? Replace them, refinish them, or simply cover them with carpeting. Does an alleyway dominate your view? Choose a window treatment that conceals it. Do you have too few closets? Buy armoires. Low ceilings? Stick with light colors. If you try to impose a decorating scheme that works against the natural bones of your home, you'll always be swimming against the current—and you may drown.

Take another walk through your home with your priority charts in hand. Note which natural assets you want to exploit and which deficits you want to downplay. You may end up moving some priorities from the *need* to the *want* column, adding some new ones, or deleting a few.

CREATE A BUDGET AND A SCHEDULE

You know exactly how much money you spend on your mortgage and car payments,

Take advantage of your house's bare bones, whether it's a family room replete with refined wood paneling and an elegant fireplace or an airy loft with original columns and exposed brick walls—whatever attracted you to your home in the first place.

how much you contribute to retirement and college funds, perhaps even how much you spend on clothes and movies and vacations. But do you have any idea how much you currently spend—or how much you *should* spend—on decorating?

Despite the importance of having a comfortable home that reflects personal style, very few people actually make the effort to *plan* for that home. Why? One possible answer is that many people consider expenditures for furniture, remodeling, or even painting to be onetime costs. Will you ever need to buy more than one sofa? How many times will you need to refinish the floors? Following this reasoning, people just don't set aside money for what they consider to be isolated expenses.

But the fact is that decorating expenditures are ongoing investments that you'll make in fits and starts throughout your life. If you don't plan your budget to accommodate these expenditures, the big-ticket items will *always* seem prohibitively expensive; you'll feel anxious before making these purchases and guilty afterward; and you'll procrastinate. By not budgeting for decorating, you compromise your budget, hamper the progress of your decorating, and add unnecessary anxiety to your life.

Turn your attention back to your room-by-room priority charts. Next to each item, put an estimate of the amount that you'll spend. If you have no idea how much an item costs, peruse the prices in catalogs or magazines. If you have no idea how much a project such as refinishing wood floors or slipcovering a sofa costs, ask your friends, family, or neighbors, or call a professional for an estimate—it's usually free.

Once you've come up with estimates, add up the figures in each *need* and *want* column, then add up the *need* and *want* totals for all rooms. Now you've arrived at the amount that you should plan on spending over a certain period of time: let's say the total of your *need* columns is $9,000, with $15,000 in your *want* columns.

Now it's time to figure out your schedule. This will depend on other aspects of your household budget, which probably includes an estimate of discretionary income. (If you haven't already created a general budget, you'll have trouble.) For instance, if you have $1,000 per month of discretionary income available and you want to spend about half of that on your home, you'll have $6,000 per year available for decorating.

With a monthly or annual budget in hand, you can return to your estimated expenses and arrive at a schedule. In the above example, with needs of $9,000 and wants of $15,000, you plan to spend $24,000; at $6,000 per year, your decorating time frame is four years.

"Oh no," you might think, "four years? I

needs, or $3,000, you'll be done with your priorities in six months. And, after all, it may take you six months just to unpack your wedding china!

Also remember that financing is possible: from home-equity loans to retailers' installment plans, there are many options that can enable you to accelerate your schedule. Be sure to shop around for the most favorable interest rates and credit programs.

DECORATING DECISIONS

You've selected an overall look, assessed your assets and deficits, determined your priorities, and set a budget and schedule. Now it's time to put the plan into action. But first, you should decide whether you want to act alone or to enlist some assistance. There are many types of people who can provide that assistance—and not just the high-profile, high-priced interior designers whose names appear regularly in the glossy magazines. Many design services are willing to provide a free consultation; retailers often offer complementary design service to help you plan your home; and designers and contractors can be found on an hourly or per-project basis, instead of a flat fee. If you think you might want professional guidance, don't hesitate to shop

can't wait four years." But before you go back to the drawing board and decide that you really don't need a vacation, remember that this budget includes both your wants *and* your needs. If you focus your attention on your needs, that $9,000 can be met in a year and a half. And during that time, you can concentrate on your most important rooms first—for most people, the living and dining rooms. So, if the needs of those two rooms add up to a third of your total

This guest room, in a rundown mountaintop retreat, seemed to have a lot in the *need* column. But after refinishing the floors, applying fresh paint, rescuing a table, and dragging in a chair from the foyer, those needs vanished into an enchanting nook.

around—you'll be pleasantly surprised to find that designers aren't just for the rich and famous.

Whether you go it alone or seek assistance, the first step is to settle on an overall look—from minimally Modernist to voluptuously Victorian, you probably already know what you want. (If not, the many styles in this book will offer inspiration.) Then it's time to get down to the fundamental decisions that will accomplish that look: treatments for floors and windows, plus the use of color throughout your home.

FLOORS

The most common floor finishes are different treatments of wood, often combined with area rugs. Before you decide what you want out of your floors, take a look at what you already have. Most residential spaces have floors made of some sort of wood. In old homes, that wood may be buried under layers of wall-to-wall carpeting or linoleum, or painted over a dozen times, but chances are that there's wood down there somewhere. A good place to look for the original flooring is in a closet.

There are a few different styles of wood floors. The most ornate is marquetry, in which a base wood is inlaid with other materials, creating a wide range of highly distinctive patterns, from repeating geometric shapes to advanced pictorial scenes. Similar to marquetry, parquetry is the arrangement of wood blocks to form geometric patterns; the pattern is provided by the placement of blocks and by the wood's natural variations in color and grain. Parquet floors in popular styles such as herringbone are readily available as easily laid premade sheets.

The most simple wood floor is made of floorboards, or planks. In general, the older floors use wider, perhaps uneven planks. Today, narrow boards with a width of only a few inches are most common.

As for the wood itself, you might find (or choose from) a wide range. Before the eighteenth century, most wood floors were

The beauty of old, wide-planked wood floors should not be hidden under rugs.

made of durable hardwoods such as oak and elm. But as supplies of hardwoods dwindled, softwoods such as fir and pine became more prevalent.

You can leave wood floors their natural color or stain them a new color. You can also paint them: from a light wash to a high-gloss saturation, from monotone to stenciling or even a trompe l'oeil adventure, the options are limited only by the bounds of your imagination. But no matter what your treatment, wood floors must be covered in a protective finish, either polyurethane or traditional wax.

Of course, if you're not fond of wood floors, there's no need to waste time on its appearance. Just take your measurements and go shopping for something else. Most often, that something else is carpeting. But gone are the days when wall-to-wall meant the orange shag in your parents' split-level. Also behind us are the days when high-maintenance, high-cost wool carpets were the only option: today, only a tiny percentage of U.S.-made carpets are pure wool. Synthetic materials such as nylon, polyester, and acrylic are less expensive, more stain-resistant, easier to clean, and longer-lasting than wool. On the other hand, these materials look and feel less luxurious, and wool takes better to dyes. But no matter what the material, the choices of color, style, pattern, and size are infinite. Whether you're looking for a casual rag rug for your kitchen or an ornate handmade Oriental to dominate your living room, you'll be able to find something to suit your vision.

Besides carpeting, the most popular non-wood options are linoleum and tile. Rubber, stone, terra-cotta, and even concrete are also possibilities. But it's a good idea to consider these very carefully: they are not only time-consuming and expensive to install, but they're also decisions you're more likely to reconsider later—the highly buffed poured-concrete that you love today is the same floor you may hate in three years.

WINDOWS

As with floors, first assess the windows themselves before you settle on your treatment: floor-to-ceiling ribbon windows will demand something entirely different than the small panes and frames of an old farmhouse.

No matter what your decor, from minimalism to opulence, you can find window treatments to enhance the look.

What's beyond the windows themselves should affect your choice of treatment. Perhaps the most obvious consideration is the view: if you have a great one, you'll want to exploit it by downplaying the treatment. If a window faces an unattractive vista or compromises your privacy, you'll want to minimize the view.

Another important consideration is natural light. If you have a lot of it, you'll probably want to take advantage of this great resource by letting in the light. But if you have too much, you'll need to provide an easy way to shield the room: too much bright light can make a room too hot (and can overwhelm an air conditioner).

You should also consider the outside noise level, which is often overlooked. If your neighborhood is particularly loud, use heavy treatments that muffle the sounds. On the other hand, if the outside noise is something you find pleasant—crashing waves, gurgling brook, singing birds—you may not want to mute the sound at all.

Finally, you should consider the real-life uses for the rooms. Are you a late riser with an east-facing bedroom? Do you eat breakfast in your underwear in a kitchen that faces the street? Are you installing window boxes or child-guards?

When you take all of these issues into consideration *and* add your taste to the mix, you might despair of too many contradictory needs pulling in opposite directions. The good news is that you can combine treatments. For example, while thick, plush, lined velvet drapes might seem to be the answer for the late riser whose bedroom looks out onto the rising sun, perhaps her decorating scheme demands a whitewashed, airy feel. The solution is a combo plan: blackout shades that can be pulled down behind sheer linen panels.

Inject color not simply through upholstery and the walls but with the judicious use of accent pieces, such as this cluster of vases.

COLOR

Last, but far from least, you'll need to choose colors. Once again the deciding factors will be the natural bones of the house combined with your personal vision.

There are many important decisions to make regarding color, but the first should concern the complexity of your scheme: Do you want a simple palette of one or two dominant colors, balanced by one or two contrasting or harmonizing colors? Or do you prefer a more complex palette? Generally speaking, your choice should reflect your overall approach to decorating: Are you aiming for soothing or stimulating? For minimalism or richness?

Then there's the question of natural versus synthetic colors: Do you want to characterize your palette with colors found in the natural world or those created by man? This issue concerns not only the colors themselves—for example, do you prefer a natural, muted moss green or a brilliant neon lime?—but also their combinations.

Once you've conceptualized your scheme, you should balance it: decide where and how to use which colors to achieve a harmonious effect. The most powerful way to introduce color in a room is on the walls, and the most common way to do this is by painting. When you choose to paint, you have many options—not just colors but also finishes (from flat to high gloss), washes, and patterns. And for a more refined, ambitious decorating statement, there is also a range of wallpapers—from simple monochromes to elaborate textured designs.

The use of color—for furniture and accents as well as walls and trim—is a subject so complex that it makes people throw up their hands and cover everything in white. But the pages that follow give you some excellent ideas about how different combinations work in different schemes. And although there may be many factors for you to weigh, the fundamental consideration should be how a color makes you *feel*. Buy a quart, slather it on a section of wall, and decide whether or not it fits your plan and your personality.

STAGES 1–2–3

Remember your ideal home? The fully furnished, fantastically finished palace of your dreams? You can achieve that look—but probably not overnight. And the trick is to make your home stylish and livable *while* you're in the process of decorating, not just at the perfect end.

A good exercise is to set three levels of goals. At the end of the chapters that follow, we've included examples of these three levels: STAGES 1–2–3. In STAGE 1, the goals are to achieve the primary use for each room—to eat in the dining room, to sleep in the bedroom—and to lay the foundation for the overall decorating scheme. In STAGE 2, the goals are to achieve the secondary uses for each room—to store china in the dining room, to talk on the telephone in the bedroom—while maintaining your focus on your intended style. In STAGE 3, the goals are to round out the decor with occasional pieces, accents, and other items that unite the scheme and make it interesting.

Most of the rooms in this book are photographed at STAGE 3, when all the decisions have been made, all the projects carried out, all the elements gathered and arranged. But if you look closely at these rooms, you'll be able to imagine the evolution from empty room to STAGE 3: refinish the floors, paint the walls, acquire the important furniture, inject more style by adding window treatments, rugs, and occasional pieces, then round out the decor with accents. To help you visualize this evolution, there are pages that outline each of the three stages—a clear path that you should replicate as you decorate your own home in stages, as your time and budget allow. In the end, you'll discover that the home you always dreamed of is, in fact, your dream come true.

STAGES 1-2-3: Begin with the bare essentials (Stage 1, top), then add some formalizing elements (Stage 2, middle), and round out with the finishing touches (Stage 3, bottom).

THE FOYER

The foyer is the transition point between the public world and your personal zone, between outdoors and indoors. Whether it's grand or barely existent, the foyer sets the tone for the rest of your home—and is, of course, the first decorating statement your guests will see. Historically, the foyer played an occasional ceremonial role in welcoming people to a home—in Victorian times, for example, when unexpected guests and gentleman callers waited patiently as their name cards were presented on silver trays to the hosts and hostesses.

These days, not many of us keep our guests cooling their heels in the entryway. But that doesn't mean the foyer has lost its sense of drama. As the point of introduction, the foyer should always be inviting, perhaps even enticing, hinting at the personalities beyond. So although many foyers are no bigger than a hallway, it's the most important hallway in the home.

STYLE AND FUNCTION

A beautiful foyer can—and should—also be deceptively practical. Here, this boldly patterned Soumak rug is useful on three fronts: its intricate pattern hides the many stains that are inevitable in the busy transition from outdoors to indoors; it can be reversed with a simple flip, which evens out wear and tear and provides two distinct decorating options; and it protects the wood in this heavily trafficked area. And, of course, the rug provides style as well as warmth and character with its strong colors.

The table arrangement is also practical, even though the most noticeable choices—such as the imposing vase of lilies, or the leather-bound books and woven balls—are completely decorative. But hiding behind these elegant statements are eminently useful details: the horizontal plane of the tabletop provides invaluable space to drop small belongings, while the basket beneath is the perfect spot for umbrellas, boots, and bags—keeping all of these things accessible but not spread out in an unruly mess.

SMART TIP IF YOU HAVE A RUG IN THE FOYER, USE A CUT-TO-FIT RUBBER MAT BENEATH IT TO PROVIDE EXTRA CUSHIONING, PROLONG THE RUG'S LIFE, AND HELP PREVENT SLIPS.

ABOVE: The strong colors of the Soumak rug are amplified by the orange-red upholstery of the cane bench. RIGHT: The table provides a great place to display unique finds—such as these antique wire hat hangers—as well as storage space on top and beneath.

Sports

GRAND ILLUSION

There's no rule that furniture in a foyer—or in any room—must be placed stiffly against the wall. In fact, in large, open rooms such as this foyer, central placements can feel much more balanced—and much less like the entrance to your dentist's office. If furniture were placed against the walls, the open space would seem cavernous and empty. But this round table and classic armchair create a focal point and a true sense of intimacy.

Central placements can be especially useful when you're in the early stages of filling a home. Just a few pieces of furniture lined up against the wall can look spartan. But in a central placement such as this one, a single table can seem to fill the room. And although this Empire-style table is refined and elegant, you could make do with a simple card or patio table hidden beneath a tablecloth. Topped with crisp linens and an artful display of objects, even such utilitarian tables can be transformed into beautiful platforms.

SMART TIP VASES AND URNS CAN HOLD MUCH MORE THAN FRESH-CUT FLOWERS—TO REFLECT THE CHANGING SEASONS, TRY DRIED FLOWERS, REEDS, OR EVEN THE SIMPLE ELEGANCE OF BARE BIRCH BRANCHES.

The natural simplicity of wood is highlighted with contrasting textures and colors: the high gloss of the cherry table, the matte surface of the bleached chair, and the honeyed hues of the oak floors, stairs, door, and banister.

THE WORKING FOYER

Inevitably, the foyer must be practical. After all, this is the spot where you shed your wet rain gear or make mud tracks when you come in from the garden.

Because the foyer is heavily trafficked, make certain that the floor covering is durable and easily cleaned. But having a functional foyer doesn't mean you have to skimp on style. For instance, if you like the classic beauty of wood flooring, just be sure to apply two or three coats of superstrong polyurethane on the sanded wood so that the shine endures and the wood is protected. Another classic choice is checkered linoleum, which offers great durability without sacrificing strong visual appeal.

Back foyers near the kitchen are adaptable to a number of creative uses—and are likely to be the most mud-attracting spot in your home. A potting shed was fashioned out of this back foyer (on the left) in a suburban New England house. You can also make such a space into a walk-in pantry, a wine "cellar," or a miniworkshop—it can, in fact, serve any of a number of practical uses.

SMART TIP PAINTED FLOORS LOOK ESPECIALLY CHARMING IN SMALL SPACES LIKE FOYERS. FOR DURABILITY, PAINT THE FLOORS IN A HIGH-GLOSS OIL-BASED PAINT AND LAYER ON THE POLYURETHANE.

LEFT: This back entryway is the perfect transition to the garden and serves as a fine potting shed. ABOVE: The handsome staircase and finial form the centerpiece of the foyer and perfectly reflect the style of this eighteenth-century farmhouse.

THE PARLOR FOYER

Bold autumnal colors embrace you the moment you step through the front door of this New York City apartment, where the foyer is a room in its own right. Loaded with old-world elegance, this space is crammed with features you might not expect in an entryway: the stately Queen Anne chest of drawers (which provides extra storage for the likes of sweaters and blankets), the antique basket cart on wheels (with a waterproof lining, perfect for umbrellas and boots), and the colored glass chandelier. The result: an entry in the guise of a parlor.

Creatively positioned flea-market finds help make great style possible on a tight budget. For instance, only the frame and upper panels remain of the eighteenth-century American screen, bought for a bargain price. But positioned in this corner behind the other pieces, you hardly notice that *most* of this screen hasn't survived—what you do notice is a charming piece. So if you find something interesting but not intact, consider some creative options before you pass it over as junk.

SMART TIP BASKETS AND BOWLS IN THE FOYER OFFER STYLISH STORAGE FOR ODDS AND ENDS AS WELL AS AN OPPORTUNITY TO SHOWCASE YOUR FAVORITE OBJECTS.

Plants in a variety of containers—especially the topiary on the floor—add hints of surprise and lushness.

THE LIVING ROOM

It's impossible to deny: the living room is the most visible room and the most important decorating statement in your home, where you impress your boss, greet out-of-town guests, or entertain your in-laws—not to mention where you spend time.

These days, though, the living room is rarely reserved just for company on special occasions. Few of us want a living room that is untouchable—a pure showpiece that's off-limits to the kids or the Labrador. For one thing, who has the space to seal off an entire room? And even if you have space to spare, chances are you want a living room that fits your everyday lifestyle—an attractive, inviting space where you can go barefoot, dive into your favorite chair, and blast the music.

Still, the living room always demands style and at least a touch of elegance. So lavish some attention and extra creativity here. This is the place to show off your style.

ARTS AND CRAFTS

A strong, handsome effect is achieved by echoing the look of the Arts and Crafts movement. Led by the aesthetic ideals of the founder of the movement, William Morris, the Arts and Crafts style evolved as a reaction against the highly ornamented creations that resulted from the mass mechanization of manufacturing in the nineteenth century —the style that we all know as Victorian. In contrast, Morris stressed the importance of natural materials; clean, well-proportioned geometry; and the absence of purely decorative adornments.

In this room, the strict Arts and Crafts aesthetic is reinterpreted to be cozier. For example, the tables and chair use gentle curves rather than the rigid horizontals that characterize the original approach, while still using the unadorned textures and colors of the natural world. But in most respects, this room is true to the original: a strong design statement, but with a modern twist.

SMART TIP TO ENSURE THAT YOUR FURNITURE GROWS WITH YOUR CHANGING NEEDS (AND BUDGET), LOOK FOR BOOKCASES THAT CAN BE ADAPTED WITH ADJUSTABLE SHELVES, AND UNITS THAT CAN BE EXPANDED, STACKED, OR REARRANGED.

The rich color and textures of the natural wood are echoed by the deep ceiling moldings and window frames.

PARAPLUIE-REVEL
The Annotated Walden
100 Years of American Newspaper Comics

SMART TIP JUST A FEW WELL-CHOSEN PIECES CAN SAY SO MUCH. WITHOUT FLOOR COVERINGS OR WINDOW TREATMENTS, WITH BARELY ANYTHING ON THE WALLS, THIS ROOM IS STILL COMPLETE—AND *VERY* SOPHISTICATED. THE FURNISHINGS ARE IN PERFECT HARMONY WITH THE APARTMENT'S BARE BONES: THE MIRRORS AND CHAIR ARMS ECHO THE SIMPLICITY OF THE FLOORS; THE LIGHT-COLORED UPHOLSTERY AND LAMPSHADE ACCENTUATE THE GLORIOUS NATURAL LIGHT; AND JUST A HANDFUL OF CAREFULLY EDITED ACCENTS SHOWCASES YOUR TASTE WITHOUT OVERWHELMING THE EYE.

DRAMATIC GESTURES

Bold colors, plush textures, and contrasting styles create pure drama in this New York City apartment. For starters, there's nothing shy about the wall color—an intoxicating shade of apple red—which is echoed in the rug, armchair, and pillow.

What ties all these strong colors together are the touches of black and deep browns: the coffee table (an antique Chinese lidded basket), the dark picture molding, the black-and-white photographs. And, of course, the black-ink calligraphy screen serves as an imposing backdrop.

Although much of the look owes a debt to traditional Chinese style—or chinoiserie, the Western interpretation—there are other influences: the blond woods suggest modern Scandinavian furniture, the metal railing on the side table is reminiscent of Art Deco, and the halogen lamp is thoroughly contemporary. Here, East and West, old and new converge beautifully.

SMART TIP USE WINDOW TREATMENTS AS A MOOD-ENHANCING DEVICE. HERE, THE FLOOR-TO-CEILING SHUTTERS NOT ONLY BLOCK OUT HARSH SUNLIGHT BUT ALSO INJECT A SENSE OF INTRIGUE, CASTING DRAMATIC SLATS OF LIGHT.

Boldness and drama can go hand in hand with ease and intimacy—this room is both striking and completely comfortable.

LEONARDO DA VINCI

THE PERSONAL TOUCH

If you are drawn to cozy, intimate settings, don't be afraid to bring personal accents into the living room. Virtually every corner of this small room is filled with items rich in sentimental value—which is what makes the space so charming and personal. A basket of knitting yarns and a needlepoint footstool betray a current hobby; old family photographs and elegant items collected from travels around the world reveal an adventurous past; and a pile of books hints at future projects.

The furniture and arrangements extend the personal touch, projecting coziness by the close proximity of the pieces to one another, and the tightly clustered assortments of vases, frames, and knickknacks. The tightly packed flowers and the warm, rich colors of the walls, upholstery, and rug round out the very boudoirlike style.

SMART TIP BIG, LAVISHLY ILLUSTRATED BOOKS, ESPECIALLY WHEN ARRANGED IN PILES, MAKE GREAT DECORATING ACCESSORIES—AS WELL AS PLEASURABLE READS, OF COURSE.

TOP: An eclectic and eloquent snapshot of the owner's rich life. ABOVE: This modest garage-sale table was dressed up with high-gloss paint. RIGHT: The big red stripes of the Roman shades add a playful note and echo the desk chair's upholstery.

Richness is in the details—the voluptuous shapes of objects on the table, the layers of interest in the glass-doored barrister's bookcase, the art that's partially obscured by curtains, even the useful storage baskets atop the arched bookcase.

THE SCENT OF SPICE

Sultry Arabian nights, the mysteries of the Casbah, and the pungent aroma of spices . . . if this is what you want to evoke, a restrained approach is probably not for you.

There's no question that rooms embellished with complex patterns and deep colors can be very seductive. Moorish-inspired interiors, such as the ones on these pages, have a particularly exotic appeal. On the left, the kilims create a richly layered composition of complex geometric patterns and traditional Moorish motifs (flora, stars, and medallions) that is simply spellbinding.

Textured surfaces also add richness and color. On the right, a remnant from an old Mexican house was made into an elongated mirror. The chipped surface of the wood, showing flecks of red paint underneath, gives the mirror a faded, rustic look that drives the room's decor. On the left, the tiled floor—which provides an indispensable cooling effect in hot climates—presents a textural contrast to the kilims, even though the colors are similar.

SMART TIP ARCHITECTURAL FRAGMENTS MAKE UNIQUE WALL DECORATIONS AND CAN OFTEN BE ADAPTED TO PRACTICAL USES SUCH AS MIRRORS, HEADBOARDS, TABLETOPS, AND TABLE BASES.

LEFT: The three different kilim patterns and the tile floor are all unified by a shared palette, and the iron bases of both the table and the lamp reinforce the cool texture of the floor. ABOVE: Both history and adventure are evoked with two unusual objects: the iron candleholder and the mirror frame made from a fragment of a Mexican house.

An old leather suitcase, peeking out from under the coffee table, not only holds magazines and books but also reinforces the sense of exotic travel that permeates the room.

SMART TIP INJECT ROMANCE AND MYSTERY WITH CANDLES IN UNEXPECTED PLACES: A SERIES OF VOTIVES ALONG A WINDOWSILL, TAPERS AND VOTIVES ON A CONSOLE, OR EVEN WALL HOLDERS.

ABOVE: Candles don't need to be formal tapers in silver candelabra—haphazardly placed votives set a more intimate scene. RIGHT: A medieval aura is created by the repetition of age-old materials—bare wood, unadorned walls, ironwork, and open flame.

CASA MEXICANA
Art of the Ancient World
CONNECTICUT
FRANK LLOYD WRIGHT

RESCUED RELICS

It's no secret that pristine, high-quality antiques are much sought after—and dearly paid for—by decorators. But the long search and high price tag don't ensure comfort or utility. You probably wouldn't sit in the Louis XIV chair that fetched five figures. And you certainly wouldn't drop flowers on it.

You won't have any compunction about tossing your flowers on this garden chair, rescued from the garage and left as is, rust and all. A single unrestored piece can project a simple, unaffected feel onto an entire room. So make sure you look around at what you already have—not just what's in your rooms, but also what's in your basement, attic, the backs of closets, garage (maybe even in your grandmother's cellar). You'll discover things you didn't even *know* you had: the antique enamel watering can that can become a beautiful vase; a family album with baby pictures of your parents, which you can extract and frame; the Fiesta ware service for eight that's been stowed since we liked Ike, for your retro fondue and Tupperware parties. Yesterday's cast-offs often become tomorrow's treasures.

SMART TIP IF A ROOM LOOKS PLAIN BECAUSE IT LACKS ARCHITECTURAL DETAILING, USE FURNITURE WITH ARCHITECTURAL FEATURES, SUCH AS THE CORNICE TOPS, ARCHES, AND COLUMNS HERE.

LEFT: A keen, creative eye found this rustic treasure hiding in the garage. ABOVE: Bookshelves aren't just for your den and your books—loaded with pictures and collections, they can be an interesting focal point of a cozy, personalized living room.

BRITISH COLONIAL CHARM

It's easy to overlook the role of textures in styling a room. Usually, we focus on colors and shapes, and completely forget about the subtle interplay of materials. But it's well worth the time to develop an eye—and feel—for the surfaces of walls, upholstery, and flooring. A mixture of smooth and rough, shiny and matte, and hard and soft surfaces add depth and complexity to a space, while uniform textures project minimalism or simplicity.

One of the best ways to add texture is to use cane, wicker, or bamboo. Not only are the furniture and accessories made in these materials affordable and readily available, but they inject exotic appeal to most any decor—the cane chairs and shapely wicker table in this room, for example, evoke the colonial elegance of the raj. Leather, of course, can provide rich texture and stately elegance. Embossed with a faux crocodile pattern, this amply proportioned sofa looks and feels luxurious, the very picture of bygone comfort and elegance.

SMART TIP ALTHOUGH SEASONING A NEW LEATHER BASEBALL MITT IS A COMPLEX PROCESS, TAKING CARE OF LEATHER FURNITURE IS A BREEZE: SIMPLY WIPE IT DOWN WITH A CLEAN CLOTH REGULARLY, AND MOP SPILLS IMMEDIATELY.

ABOVE: The tufted ottoman is practical and stylish: it serves as coffee table, footrest, and extra seating all in one. RIGHT: The pale colors, delicate stems, and minimal foliage of orchids add subtle elegance without clashing with the room's palette.

SMART TIP LEATHER UPHOLSTERY, STRONG AND DURABLE, COMES IN A RANGE OF COLORS AND TEXTURES. FOR A SOPHISTICATED, CONTEMPORARY LOOK, SMOOTH BLACK LEATHER IS UNMATCHED; FOR A GENTLY AGED EFFECT, TRY GRAINED LEATHER. BUT IN EITHER CASE, THE STRENGTH OF A HIGH-QUALITY PIECE CAN LAST A LIFETIME—AND LONGER.

A British Colonial side table (right) is one of the many details that provide a cohesive style: from the early-twentieth-century fan and the leather frames to the bamboo shades and alligator-grained sofa, every item evokes the same era.

THE CHARMS OF NEW ENGLAND

Tucked away on a country road, this 1874 house in Milton, Massachusetts, is distinctly American inside and out. Both the architecture and the furnishings are unassuming and understated, ever faithful to the house's New England heritage—a traditional look, albeit one that doesn't sacrifice the comfort and practicalities of today.

But traditional doesn't mean boring, as this elegantly appointed room proves. While the materials and color scheme are simple, great care is taken to coordinate accents: note how the brass drawer pull of the Federal side table echoes the base of the lamp. Even more significant, the stenciled wallpaper picks up a similar pattern on the covered urn, and both relate to the natural patterns of the cleanly framed botanical prints, which in turn echo the rosemary topiary, potted hyacinth, and vase of flowers. In fact, everything in the room relates to something else—even to the surrounding landscape.

SMART TIP A HISTORICAL LOOK IS IN THE DETAILS: FOR EXAMPLE, THE LIGHTING EMPHASIS IS ON NATURAL LIGHT, AND THE LAMP IS A CANDLESTICK DESIGN THAT'S TRUE TO COLONIAL STYLE; TRACK LIGHTING OR A HALOGEN TORCHÈRE WOULDN'T WORK.

LEFT: A wing chair, originally designed to shield the sitter from drafts, is tucked into a cozy corner. ABOVE: The dark window frames are a perfect example of the restrained beauty that is typical of New England architectural details.

SMART TIP COFFEE TABLES AREN'T THE ONLY POSSIBLE CENTERPIECES FOR SEATING ARRANGEMENTS. OTTOMANS, BENCHES, OR TEA TABLES SUCH AS THESE ARE INTERESTING, MORE FLEXIBLE OPTIONS. FOR EXAMPLE, THESE TABLES CAN BE MOVED AND THEIR LEAVES OPENED TO PROVIDE MUCH-NEEDED SURFACES FOR A BUFFET COCKTAIL PARTY.

ABOVE: This pair of Josephine chairs, covered in striped cotton, has a clean elegance that would fit in many decorating schemes.
RIGHT: Two Chippendale-style tea tables in cherry are placed in front of the camelback settee.

DANCE AND PHOTOGRAPHY
Pablo PICASSO
JESSE McDONALD
ART
ART
THE WORLD of ART
Van Gogh
MEYER SCHAPIRO

A TRIO OF SOFAS

Without doubt, your choice of sofa is one of the more important decisions in the entire house. It drives the decor of the whole room, and a sofa that doesn't match the other elements makes everything look out of place.

Some sofas have such distinct constructions that they can never be adapted for a different look—think of Le Corbusier's rectangular sofa with exposed tubular supports. Although you can replace its traditional black leather upholstery with a warm print, or you can refinish the chrome tubes in gold tones, you're never going to end up with a sofa that's anything but Modernist.

On the other hand, other sofas are infinitely flexible. The three rooms shown here are, in fact, all the same room, but with markedly different decor. Furthermore, the three sofas are the same exact sofa, but with different fabrics for the upholstery, different pillows, and different treatments for the skirting. Without sacrificing solid construction or high style, it's possible to buy furniture with unlimited flexibility.

SMART TIP IT'S NOT JUST THE OVERALL SHAPE OF A SOFA THAT DETERMINES ITS STYLE, BUT ALSO THE FABRIC (COLOR, PATTERN, AND TEXTURE), THE SKIRTING, AND THE PILLOWS. WHEN SHOPPING, USE YOUR IMAGINATION TO DESIGN YOUR IDEAL SOFA.

LEFT: An unskirted sofa and isolated touches of color define this clean-lined Modernist room. TOP: The kick-pleat skirt provides a more classical treatment. ABOVE: Transformation to an unabashedly country look is achieved with a gathered skirt.

SEA BREEZE

Sea-foam greens and pale blues are as calming as a day by the sea—merely enter a room decorated in this palette, and you will feel your blood pressure drop instantly. Close your eyes and you can almost hear the sound of waves washing along a deserted beach, feel fine-grained sand beneath your feet.

This home in Houston, Texas, is a good distance from water, but it has the look and feel of an old-fashioned beach house. The dark brown furniture prevents the room from looking monotonous and overly coordinated, but the overall effect is unmistakably light and casual; the soft colors, lacy curtains, and neutral-colored rug create a breezy look that's at once casual and elegant.

The focal point is the whitewashed screen, inspired by wooden shutters from an American Gothic church. Not only does the screen enhance the summer mood, but it partitions the room, providing both openness and privacy in the same space.

SMART TIP RUGS MADE FROM SISAL, COIR, OR SEA GRASS GIVE ROOMS A SUMMERY LOOK, NO MATTER WHAT THE SEASON OR LOCALE. YOU CAN CREATE THE SAME LOOK WITH WOVEN WOOL RUGS THAT WEAR AND CLEAN EXTREMELY WELL.

Fresh flowers, basket boxes, and old apothecary jars on a pedestal table impart an unstuffy, old-fashioned feel.

un vrai moutard
c'est un poulbot
une vraie moutarde
c'est :
A MOUTARDE
ARIZOT
BISCUITS
PERNOT
ANATOMY FOR
THE ARTIST

RED REDUX

Robust reds, vivid chartreuse, and strong yellows are not for the faint of heart. But applied judiciously, these colors deliver a knockout punch to an ordinary living room—and create a truly unforgettable space.

The room on the left has a distinctly French flavor, provided most noticeably by the bright, lively colors that are typical of the Continental approach: strong colors applied without hesitation or fear. In the rear dining alcove, note the two different wallpapers and the third pattern for the curtains—all complementary, but hardly matching. And the nineteenth-century chest and advertising posters provide the links to the past that are so present in European households.

On the other hand, the room on the right is distinctly American. The visible water pipe, exposed brick walls, planked-wood floor, and paned windows are all elements of residential lofts that have been converted from old manufacturing buildings—a typically American history of preserving the heritage of the Industrial Revolution.

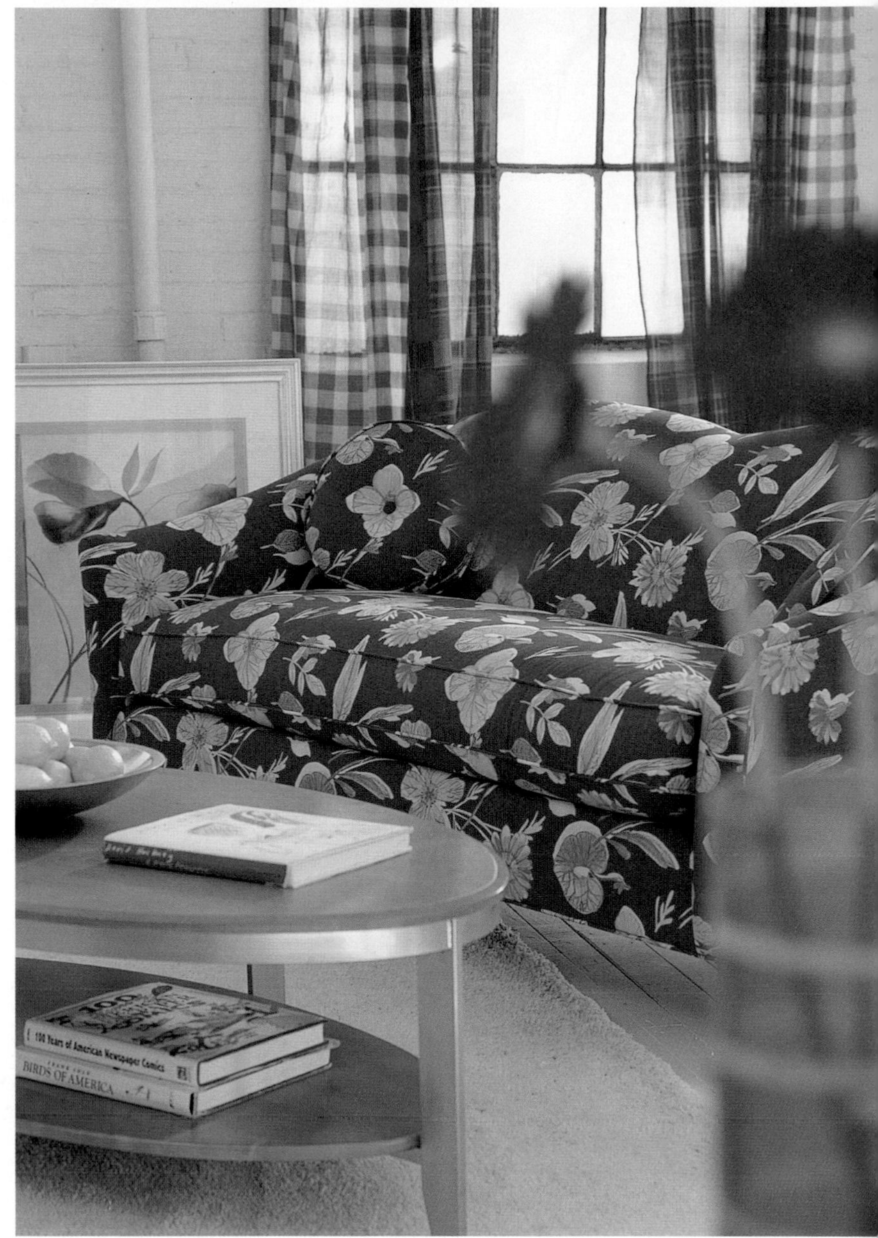

SMART TIP **ADVERTISING POSTERS—EITHER REPRODUCTIONS OR ORIGINALS—ARE OFTEN GREAT REPRESENTATIVES OF ERAS OR DESIGN STYLES (SUCH AS ART DECO, ART NOUVEAU, BAUHAUS, AND POP ART), AND MAKE UNIQUE DECORATING ACCENTS.**

LEFT: This beautiful antique chest is an eminently practical coffee table, providing not only a horizontal surface but also ample storage room. ABOVE: The floral motif is echoed in the cut flowers and the floral poster, tying together the whole room.

PARED-DOWN ELEGANCE

With the right approach, a neutral palette can be an element of many decorating approaches. In the Connecticut home on the left, the furniture styles and architecture are all unabashedly traditional, but the neutral tones ensure a clean, modern feel that makes this anything but ordinary suburbia.

On the right, the neutral walls reinforce the urban chic of this loft in TriBeCa, New York—definitely not Connecticut. The loft feel is often accomplished by retaining the space's industrial look—hand-operated freight elevators, exposed sprinklers, bare brick walls. But the same feel can be approximated in nearly any home by eliminating the formal adornments of a fine residence. Here, note the wall's lack of moldings and its almost concrete-looking color and texture; the oak plank floors (rather than parquet) were allowed to scuff naturally, rather than be buffed to the high gleam that was used in the Connecticut house. With the same floors and the same color scheme, the two homes take on totally different looks.

SMART TIP DIFFERENT APPROACHES TO DISPLAYING ART CREATE TOTALLY DIFFERENT FEELS. AT RIGHT, THE FINELY FRAMED BUT UNHUNG DRAWING IS REMINISCENT OF A GALLERY'S INSTALLATION-IN-PROGRESS. ON THE OTHER HAND, THIS SAME PIECE, SPOTLIT AND HUNG DIRECTLY AT SIGHT LINE IN THE CENTER OF THIS LARGE, NEUTRAL WALL, WOULD PRODUCE A MORE FORMAL EFFECT.

OSCAR
OSCAR WILDE
Van Gogh

STAGES 1-2-3

STAGE 1 Although the walls are unadorned, the windows untreated, and the floors bare, this room is livable because the defining pieces are in place: a traditional two-seat sofa paired with an upholstered dining chair and round side table satisfy all needs.

STAGE 2 A more formal, finished look is created by adding damask wall coverings, matching Roman shades, and an Aubusson rug.

STAGE 3 Finally, the small table is moved to the side, and more substantial pieces, such as the velvet slipper chair and the coffee table, assume their rightful places.

ALFRED STIEGLITZ
The COMPLETE ETCHINGS of GOYA
CONNECTICUT

THE FAMILY ROOM

More akin to Grand Central Station than an island of calm, the family room hums with activity day and night: the kids and neighbors traipse in and out, the television blares, and the pet iguana is loose. Chaos is an inherent trait, and it's futile to try to resist it; instead, embrace the informality and plan your scheme with the realities of day-to-day life in mind. Because the family room serves so many functions for so many people, comfort and practicality must be top priorities. Furniture, rugs, and upholstery should be tough enough to withstand the wear and tear of everyday use, not to mention some serious abuse—from roughhousing on the sofa to paw prints on the rugs.

Practical considerations aside, a stylish decor is still essential—after all, this is where the family spends most of their waking hours, so whatever gives you a sense of home will work. Just remember: this is the room for casual living.

THE HIDEAWAY

Wood isn't just wood—it's oak or ash, pine or cherry, mahogany or ebony. Each wood has different properties: color, of course, is the most noticeable variation, but woods also have markedly different degrees of hardness or softness, prominence of grain, and presence of knots. And all of these details contribute to the overall look of a room. Light or blond woods, for instance, are the predominant choice in Scandinavian design and many modern styles, and they impart a decidedly contemporary look with their cool, neutral colors and subtle grain.

Here, the choice of knotty pine sets a casual tone for both rooms. The room on the left is paneled in horizontal, wide-width planks—*very* informal, like a hunting lodge or ski house. On the right, the pine is limited to the impressive mantelpiece, whose detailed architecture provides a bit of formality. But the warm color, soft density, and natural imperfections of knotty pine ensure that both rooms are cozy, inviting you to sink into the plush chair or sofa in your pajamas.

SMART TIP NOT ONLY IS THERE A VAST CHOICE OF WOODS BUT ALSO OF FINISHES*:* SATIN, GLOSS, AND HIGH-GLOSS POLYURETHANES, EITHER OIL- OR WATER-BASED, NOT TO MENTION GOOD OLD WAX.

ABOVE: The irregularity of fieldstone floors and the knotty pine make this a truly casual, natural room. RIGHT: Despite the rustic look of the pine, this mantelpiece is slightly formalized by the symmetrical, uncluttered arrangement of objects across the top.

ROTTERDAM
DEGAS
CONNECTICUT
DANCE AND PHOTOGRAPHY

AN ATTIC WITHOUT COBWEBS

The family room doesn't need to be on the first floor, formally positioned between the living and dining rooms. You can carve a pleasant, useful gathering spot out of many spaces: a spare bedroom, the basement, the garage, or an attic such as this one. Because of the tight space, furniture and color selection were kept simple. For small or low-ceilinged rooms, it's usually a good bet to keep the range of colors and number of furniture pieces to a minimum, or you might end up with a cluttered look.

For furnishing rooms that you don't intend to use for many different purposes—for example, this second family room, used mainly for reading—it's important not to forget your goal. If you begin decorating by immediately accomplishing that goal—get a comfortable couch and appropriate lighting—you've succeeded right from the start. Of course, you can add occasional pieces and expand the decorating scheme, but on a leisurely schedule and without breaking your budget.

SMART TIP **TO MAXIMIZE STORAGE SPACE IN SMALL QUARTERS, USE LOW CHESTS OF DRAWERS AS FLEXIBLE, MOBILE, AND EMINENTLY PRACTICAL SIDE TABLES.**

A wool rug in a natural hue helps insulate against noise and gives warmth and coziness to this attic family room.

RED HOT

For a striking design statement, never underestimate the power of unusual shapes and materials—a single piece in an unexpected form can make a whole room truly bold. This Tampa Bay family room is arranged conventionally with comfortable, traditional shapes for the couch and armchair, white walls, and wood floors covered in serene rugs. And yet . . . there's something unmistakably bold that sets this room apart and creates a sense of style and drama.

That something is unexpected shapes: the triangular clock, playing against the rectangles of the art and books; the spiral pattern of the nickel-plated side chair; the sharp diagonal angle of the halogen lamp; and the overlapping circles of the end table. The surprising shapes mixed with the traditional forms create a striking, contemporary look that's anything but ordinary.

And tying the whole room together is bright, lively red—not just the vivid couch, but the trim on the window shades, the accents in the upholstered English-style armchair, the art, even the leather-bound books on the mantel.

SMART TIP FLOWERS NEEDN'T BE FORMALLY ARRANGED IN A FLUTED ETCHED-CRYSTAL VASE. TRY TALL COCKTAIL PITCHERS, A SET OF HIGHBALLS, OR THESE WHIMSICAL PINT GLASSES.

ABOVE: The hot, bright colors and shapes of the mantelpiece and the sofa project warmth to the entire room. RIGHT: The natural vertical lines of windows are reinforced by the red stripes of the linen Roman shades and the tall curio cabinet between the windows.

CLEAN LINES

Clean lines are usually associated with the stark, often uncomfortable minimalism that's been so visible in recent years. But as these two rooms prove, clean lines can contribute to eminently livable spaces. Though one is infused with warm light and the other is permeated by cool tones, both project a relaxed, contemplative mood.

In both, basic shapes and unfussy arrangements dominate. On the left, the linear geometry of the coffee table, side table, and cabinet echo the diamond-patterned upholstery of the chair and the simple shapes of the pottery; the display cabinet, with square insets in the wood and glass, reflects the simply treated windows.

On the right, cool colors and natural textures create an effect as tranquil as a rock garden. Taupe walls, neutral canvas upholstery, and dark wicker and wood give a harmonious, relaxed feeling. And the accent colors only add to the serenity: pale blue pillows and celadon ceramics inject color without compromising the muted palette.

SMART TIP DON'T UNDERESTIMATE THE POWER OF WINDOW TREATMENTS TO SET A ROOM'S TONE: FROM UTTER SIMPLICITY TO OUTRIGHT EXTRAVAGANCE, THE WINDOWS SHOULD HARMONIZE WITH THE OTHER ELEMENTS OF YOUR STYLE.

LEFT: The sofa and chair were upholstered in different patterns but in the same color scheme and with the same scale—not strictly matching but a cohesive pair. ABOVE: The rug's pattern adds definition to the seating area and stresses the clean lines.

PICASSO
Art in

A mix of country-inspired patterns and clean, modern lines keep this family room true to its rural roots but with a modern spirit.

COUNTRY CHARMS

Country style no longer means frumpy upholstery, outdated appliances, or Granny's rocking chairs. Now country decor has a simpler, more sophisticated air for modern sensibilities and needs.

In this rural home, the bare bones of the house—the floors and fireplace—and the checkered upholstery are the main elements that define the country style. But there's nothing cluttered or dowdy about it—in fact, most of the choices here reflect a thoroughly modern eye, especially in the accents. The windows, for instance, are treated with sheer, clean-looking panels, rather than a heavy gingham or damask. The walls are painted a soft, cool slate instead of the pastels or bright primaries that adorn many farmhouses. And the single piece of art is whimsically displayed on an easel, not hung on the wall amid the typical collection of family photos.

SMART TIP SHOWCASE WONDERFUL WOOD FLOORS, AN IMPRESSIVE FIREPLACE, OR EVEN JUST GREAT NATURAL LIGHT WITH THE EASIEST TREATMENTS: BASIC SHEER PANELS FOR WINDOWS, A SMALL AREA RUG, A BARELY ACCESSORIZED MANTELPIECE . . . THE SIMPLEST CHOICES CAN BE THE BEST ONES.

BIG SKY DREAMS

The imposing stone fireplace, two stories high, is the centerpiece of this dramatic double-height room. To accentuate the magnificent height, the huge windows were kept bare, offering wonderful light and sweeping vistas of the surrounding countryside, glorious mornings and spectacular sunsets.

The furniture and decorations follow the grand scale with generous proportions: the sofa is wide and deep, with ample roll arms and pillows; the English-style side chair is big and embracing. A large, square coffee table with drawers anchors the seating arrangement. And the connection to the outdoors is reinforced with the fully planted window box (albeit in the fireplace), the watering can, and the weather vane.

SMART TIP WHILE LADDERS HAVE THEIR OBVIOUS UTILITARIAN ROLES, THEY CAN ALSO SERVE AS UNUSUAL ACCENTS. HERE, AN ANTIQUE'S DISTRESSED FINISH MAKES A PERFECT SHOWCASE FOR VINTAGE QUILTS. BUT AN INEXPENSIVE HARDWARE-STORE LADDER, STAINED A RICH CHERRY AND FINISHED WITH A HIGH GLOSS, COULD BE A SOPHISTICATED TIERED PEDESTAL FOR VASES AND BOOKS.

In the most harmonious country-style decorating, the beauty of the natural world is reflected inside.

DECORATING
The Old Barn Book

INTO THE WOODS

Fashioned out of an old carriage house in coastal Maine, this cottage is the summer retreat of a Boston family. In keeping with the structure's rustic character, some of the furniture was recycled from old barns or homes in the nearby countryside. For example, the wrought-iron glass-top coffee table, the side table, and the child's chair all date back to the 1920s. In these instances, restoration consisted of nothing more than some rough sanding and a quick coat of white paint, which could all be accomplished in a few hours. The imperfections —dried paint chips and uneven surfaces— are part of their charm and heritage .

The new additions to this room are the wicker chair, red-and-white cotton rug, and red-check slipcovers on the sofa—all inexpensive and easy. During the off-season, the summer slipcovers come off and are replaced with heavy denim; Hudson Bay blankets emerge, and a roaring fire is lit.

SMART TIP COFFEE TABLES DON'T NEED TO BE LOW-TO-THE-GROUND AFFAIRS WITHIN EASY REACH OF TODDLERS' HANDS OR DOGS' TAILS. A LARGE, HIGH TABLE CAN SERVE PERFECTLY *AND* DO DOUBLE DUTY AS A MAKESHIFT DINING OR GAME TABLE.

The walls in this carriage house were painted a deep chocolate to hide imperfections; wainscoting makes the ceiling less cavernous.

STAGES 1-2-3

STAGE 1 With a minimum of sturdy pieces this room is comfortable and relaxing.

STAGE 2 When decorating in stages, don't discard pieces once you've upgraded; plan new uses for old pieces. The folding tables are now doing duty to balance the corner.

STAGE 3 An entertainment unit can be a significant choice—and an expensive investment. Here, the family started with just the bare essential—a sturdy piece to house the television, VCR, and stereo. But they chose the piece for its adaptability, and so had the freedom to add on these wings of bookshelves.

MARSEILLE
PORTE DE L'AFRIQUE DU NORD

STAGES 1-2-3

STAGE 1 Make your important choices first and carefully, and you'll be able to add pieces with a clear mission and very little stress: here, the coordination of the sofa's upholstery and the walls will define this room through many other additions and changes.

STAGE 2 Adding rugs is a quick, easy, and often inexpensive way to make a room much homier, especially with low-cost items such as a cotton rug or smaller runners and area rugs.

STAGE 3 A "proper" coffee table takes the place of the bench that was called into service, and a larger rug pulls the room together.

THE DINING ROOM

Although the dining room's primary purpose is incredibly straightforward—simply a place to eat—it's also a room imbued with deeper contexts and purposes: both a private family spot and a public gathering point for friends and colleagues; to serve an easy microwave dinner or to lay out a holiday feast for the whole extended family; for quick breakfasts, languid weekend lunches, or a Sunday-night roast. And perhaps a jigsaw puzzle in between.

Living rooms and family rooms are often used for solitary activities: reading, watching a movie, doing homework—each member of the family doing his or her own thing. But in the dining room, everyone's doing the same things: eating and talking. In virtually all cultures, gathering around a table for a meal remains a powerful family ritual and an unequivocal gesture of goodwill and inclusion—all the more so in a stylish space.

JEWEL BOX ELEGANCE

For many apartment dwellers, it's rare to have an entire room devoted to dining. But with a bit of space planning, you can carve an intimate dining area out of your living room, kitchen, or even a hallway.

In this one-bedroom apartment in San Francisco's Nob Hill, a corner of the foyer serves perfectly. Sunlight permeates the entire space, so this small area never feels confining. A large mirror gives a greater sense of depth—a tried-and-true technique for visually expanding nearly any room.

Though this spot is tight, the decor is neither cramped nor spartan, and it's certainly not wimpy. Strong shapes and high contrast provide definition: the turned baluster legs, the thick frames, the huge candles and oversize vase of cherry blossoms. In a small room, you might want to choose small, noncommittal furnishings, but as this nook proves, the opposite approach makes for a much more dramatic design.

SMART TIP IF SPACE—OR THE LACK OF IT—IS A PRIME CONSIDERATION, LOOK FOR EXPANDABLE (AND HENCE SHRINKABLE) TABLES: THOSE WITH REMOVABLE LEAVES OR SOFA TABLES WITH FLIP-OUT TOPS, SUCH AS THIS ONE.

A small space can still be elegant—this portion of the hallway, no larger than a good-sized closet, makes a perfect dining nook.

SMART TIP THE ONLY *ESSENTIAL* ELEMENTS TO A DINING ROOM ARE THE TABLE AND CHAIRS, SO START DECORATING WITH WISE CHOICES HERE. BEGIN WITH A TABLE THAT YOU'LL BE ABLE TO ENJOY FOR YEARS TO COME, AND MAKE DO WITH FOLDING CHAIRS IF NEED BE, MANY OF WHICH CAN BE DRESSED UP WITH EASY AND INEXPENSIVE SLIPCOVERS. ADD MATCHING (OR COMPLEMENTARY) CHAIRS AS YOUR BUDGET ALLOWS, THEN A SIDEBOARD, CREDENZA, OR BREAKFRONT.

Despite a minimal number of pieces, this room achieves a fully decorated look because of the high style and classic elegance of the furniture.

AN INVITING NOOK

There's no dedicated dining room in this modest eighteenth-century farmhouse. But in typical farmhouse style, the kitchen is amply proportioned, with all of the appliances grouped together at one end of the room. A butcher-block island in the middle provides the perfect divider to create this charming nook that's far from cramped.

In a relatively small space such as this, it's best to stick with the essentials: a classic farmhouse table and some chairs. Here, the owners also needed an armoire to store their china, crystal, and linens, because this old house doesn't boast the built-in kitchen cabinets that became de rigeur in the following century. The distressed finish of this piece is enhanced by the collection of antique rolling pins that hang from simple nails, and the heavily patinated copper weathervane on top. And although the general style is decidedly rustic farmhouse, a touch of elegance is introduced by the chandelier. The overall effect is cohesive without becoming belabored.

SMART TIP TO ENHANCE THE PERIOD LOOK OF A ROOM, SEEK OUT HARDWARE THAT MATCHES THE STYLE. HERE, THE WROUGHT-IRON DOOR HINGES ARE ORIGINAL TO THE HOUSE. BUT ANTIQUES AND REPRODUCTIONS CAN BE FOUND FOR ANY PERIOD.

ABOVE: These pieces, in different colors and styles, are united by the swirling texture of the pottery. RIGHT: The unified color scheme and rustic textures are a perfect match to this colonial-era farmhouse and to the natural palette of the surrounding countryside.

THE GREAT ROOM

By design, this home doesn't have a separate dining room. The owners of this midwestern ranch-style house decided that the adjoining living and dining rooms in the original plan were too small for their tastes. So for a more open, airy feel, they knocked down the wall between the rooms to create a sprawling great room. In the rear is this dining area, which also boasts a comfortable chair by the fireplace, as well as a classic writing desk—combining the living room, dining room, family room, and home office in one.

To avoid a cluttered, haphazard look that can result from multiuse spaces, everything is tied together with warm hues and classic forms. The furniture woods pair perfectly with the honey of the oak floor and the brick fireplace. And the warmth is reinforced through accents such as the silver-plated coffee urn and ice bucket, the brass andirons, and the redware bowls.

SMART TIP IF YOU FEEL HEMMED IN BY SMALL ROOMS, CONSIDER KNOCKING DOWN A WALL TO CREATE LARGER SPACES—NOT ONLY FOR SUCH PAIRINGS AS LIVING AND DINING ROOMS, BUT ALSO TO CREATE A LARGE MASTER SUITE OUT OF TWO SMALLISH BEDROOMS.

Warmth is infused through every detail, from the yellows of the wall and upholstery to the reddish woods throughout.

PURE AND SIMPLE

For cool, classic elegance, it's hard to beat the combination of white, green, and unadorned wood, which evokes natural lushness but also purity and cleanness. When the owners moved into this house, they were on a tight budget. So instead of filling the house with furniture immediately, they concentrated on establishing the predominating style through the color scheme and judicious purchases.

They started by refinishing the walls. The wainscoting had been the naturally dark oak, and the walls had been papered in a rich, saturated red—very reminiscent of a gentleman's library. So they whitewashed the wood, stripped the paper, and painted the walls avocado.

The first furniture choices were simply the elegant table and chairs—all they really needed for a dining room. As time passed, they replaced a no-nonsense light fixture with the wrought-iron chandelier, then added a sideboard in the same style and colors as the other furniture, and finally a rug in the same palette.

SMART TIP TO CREATE A COHESIVE LOOK, USE A LIMITED ARRAY OF COLORS FOR YOUR ACCENTS, SUCH AS THE WHITE AND GREEN HERE. OTHER THAN THE NATURAL WOOD AND THE GOLD-LEAF FRAME, THERE'S BARELY ANOTHER COLOR IN THE ROOM.

LEFT: A simple, unified palette combined with a judicious choice of furniture and an abundance of accents make this room striking.

ABOVE: The color scheme continues in the adjoining hallway, a small space made useful as a place to store china and linen.

THE FORMAL DINING ROOM

Despite the informality of modern times and the hectic pace of life, there will always be a place for the traditional formal dining room. Though not necessarily as grand or imposing as it once was, such a room can still carry a sense of dignified ritual.

Both rooms on these pages reflect the hallmarks of the formal eating salon. To begin with, note the walls' architectural elements: chair-height wainscoting on the left and eye-level coffered paneling on the right, suffusing the rooms with an air of propriety. Next, note the wood—mahogany, the classic choice for fine English dining furniture. Buffed to a high shine, mahogany goes beautifully with crystal, silver, and china, richly reflecting their luster.

Fine china displayed in a breakfront further enhances the formal mood, especially when the furniture is ornately carved mahogany. Finally, the use of upholstery for the chairs completes the air of civilization. There's nothing rigid or uncomfortable about either of these rooms—quite the contrary, in fact—but they both adhere to the classic tradition of the formal dining room.

SMART TIP WHILE A FULL STERLING SERVICE IS NICE, FLEA MARKETS, GARAGE SALES, AND EVEN ANTIQUES DEALERS OFFER INCOMPLETE SETS AND MISMATCHED PIECES THAT ARE FAR LESS EXPENSIVE.

To achieve true elegance, even rooms appointed with richly colored walls, high pieces of furniture, and wainscoting or paneling need some wall adornments; a pair of prints or some pieces of heirloom china serve perfectly.

This lettuce-green dining room looks bright and fresh even on the coldest New England morning. Set in the bucolic hills of Fairfield County, Connecticut, this old farmhouse serves as the weekend refuge for a busy New York couple, their three terriers, and a never-ending stream of weekend guests—all of them more than content to spend endless hours nibbling and sipping at an inviting table.

Because the dining room serves as a central gathering place, the owners wanted a relaxing, easily maintained, but still stylish space. So they chose a breathable color—this strikingly fresh green. But to balance the brightness and prevent the room from being loud, the cupboard and chairs are stained a muted gray-blue. The decor is light and relaxed, but the mood of the room is far from nonchalant—the perfect space in which to spend the weekend with good friends.

SMART TIP IF YOUR TASTES RUN TOWARD THE SUBTLE AND UNDERSTATED, YOU MAY WINCE AT DECORATING A CHRISTMAS TREE WITH THE TYPICAL TRAPPINGS: STRINGS OF ELECTRIC LIGHTS, MULTICOLORED GLOBES, AND CERAMIC FIGURINES. FOR A MORE RESTRAINED TREE, TRY THIS MONOCHROMATIC APPROACH.

The vibrancy of these walls is perfectly set off by the muted palette of the furniture and the profusion of whites.

WARM AND WELCOMING

Ochers, peach tones, and mellow yellows cast a warm glow in almost any dining room. Add a few strokes of apple red, deep orange, or chestnut brown, and the result is a room that is exceptionally welcoming.

Everything about this suburban Michigan dining room exudes a sense of the casual country life. From the bowls of fresh produce and the different sets of ceramics to the farmhouse-style table and the Shaker-inspired chairs, every detail underscores the lack of pretension that makes the country life—and country decor—universally appealing. Even the finishes to the furniture—simple beeswax for the pine-top table and soft black paint for the chairs—are true to roots.

But to avoid a look that projects incompletion or carelessness, don't neglect the small details that can add so much to a room: even simple curtains make a tremendous difference; a grouping of pottery (perhaps only two pieces) instead of a single piece creates a collection; and some flowers or a potted plant provides a welcome dose of hospitality.

SMART TIP A DAILY DELIVERY OF FRESHLY CUT IMPORTED FLOWERS IS, WITHOUT QUESTION, AN EXTRAVAGANT INDULGENCE. FOR A MORE REASONABLE APPROACH TO BRINGING A BIT OF NATURE INDOORS, LOOK TO YOUR KITCHEN FOR THE BEAUTY OF FRESH PRODUCE.

Both bold and inviting, the wall colors in these rooms contrast perfectly with the matching greens of the pottery and the window's frame and shutters (LEFT) and is warmly complemented by the red of the curtains (RIGHT).

ZEN PALATE

Japanese and Shaker aesthetics converge in this suburban Virginia dining room. Simple geometry and the beauty of natural wood define the furniture. But although the lines are clean and uncluttered, this furniture is not plain—the recessed panels on the armoire, for instance, are purely decorative, but in the restrained fashion typical of the Shaker style. And this same armoire is highly functional, fitted with drawers that are perfect for silverware and odds and ends, and shelves that are perfect for a stereo, dinnerware, or even a collection of vases.

The judicious choice of accents reinforces the calm simplicity of both styles: the unadorned windows; the neutral linen wallpaper, chair upholstery, and carpet; the modern design of the light fixture. Even the artwork—a charcoal drawing in broad strokes—is true to the aesthetic ideal. This room is definitely not for the flea-market hound who could never have too many country antiques. Instead, the result is a pure serenity—the perfect antidote to a hectic workday.

SMART TIP AN ENDLESSLY VERSATILE ARMOIRE IS THE STORAGE SOLUTION TO ALMOST ANY PROBLEM—FROM A TELEVISION, STEREO, OR BLANKETS TO VASES, CHINA, AND SILVER.

LEFT: For unfussy elegance, nothing beats the beauty of natural wood, here in a dark walnut. ABOVE: A collection of Modernist- and Japanese-inspired ceramics looks out onto a room with the same heritage.

STAGES 1-2-3

STAGE 1 Start with the essentials: for a dining room, you need nothing more than a table and chairs. Here, the color scheme is established with the wallpaper and curtains, and the functionality is accomplished with a mahogany table and Chippendale chairs.

STAGE 2 Touches of elegance are added with a chandelier, area rug, and credenza, as well as with the small lamps and mirror.

STAGE 3 A full, formal dining room is rounded out with a richly detailed breakfront that displays heirloom china and creates a striking focal point.

THE KITCHEN

Sooner or later, everyone ends up in the kitchen. Whether at a subdued dinner for a few close friends or a rowdy cocktail party for a hundred, the kitchen draws a crowd like no other room in the house. Without doubt, food is one of the big lures—not just the enticing aroma of a slow-cooked stew, but also the associations: of doing homework on the table, of hurried breakfasts and slow dinners and late-night snacks by the light of the refrigerator.

Intentionally or not, much of family life takes place in the kitchen, so it has to be comfortable and inviting. But it must also perform with maximum efficiency, not just for cooking, cleaning, and eating, but also for bringing in the groceries, taking out the trash, leaving messages, sorting mail, feeding the dog... perhaps the majority of household tasks. And for all this activity, a well-organized, well-designed space can make all the difference between an annoying chore and a pleasant diversion, and between efficiency and a mess.

COUNTRY COOKING

American farmhouse kitchens are always in vogue—warm and inviting, basic and honest. But rustic or antique styles can be a challenge to utilitarian rooms that rely on modern technology as much as contemporary kitchens do.

In this kitchen, the unassuming antique table, pine cabinetry, and red-brick flooring project comfort and tranquility. And the tone set by the major choices is supported by the details—the candle chandelier, wire baskets, and traditional redware pottery all enhance the country antique look and create a welcoming atmosphere.

But don't be deceived by the rustic airs. This kitchen is stocked with modern conveniences—they're just discreetly hidden. For instance, fluorescent lights are installed underneath the cabinets. The dishwasher (which no one would want to sacrifice for the sake of decor) is paneled in the same pine as the cabinetry, so it's barely noticeable. And those old-fashioned-looking cabinets are actually brand new. Antique style without antique headaches.

SMART TIP MODERN CONVENIENCES NEED NOT ENTAIL REJECTING A PERIOD OR RUSTIC LOOK. DISHWASHERS, STOVES, AND REFRIGERATORS CAN ALL BE OUTFITTED TO MATCH A PARTICULAR SCHEME; LIGHTS CAN BE RECESSED; AND APPLIANCES CAN BE HIDDEN.

ABOVE: These European country–inspired ceramics, artfully grouped together on the windowsill, provide a homey touch without blocking the view. RIGHT: Unpainted wooden surfaces and cabinetry contribute to the rustic, country look.

PROFESSIONAL POSHNESS

This perfectly appointed kitchen is designed for a serious cook. The professional stove delivers high, restaurant-worthy heat that home ranges just can't achieve, and the large hood vents the inevitable steam and smoke from that high heat. Cooking utensils hang exactly where they're needed—above the stove, which also accommodates storage for the most commonly used ingredients.

Besides a good knife and a decent stove, what every chef needs is more counter space—and this kitchen doesn't skimp on it. The countertops around the perimeter are topped with white Carrara marble, while the center island is capped with a slab of moss-green marble. Not only do the countertops provide ample surfaces for prepping ingredients, they also provide invaluable space for depositing groceries, polishing silver, repairing that cracked vase, or any number of household tasks.

SMART TIP CREATE SPACE THAT CAN ACCOMMODATE LARGE ITEMS, SUCH AS BASKETS, SERVING PLATTERS, AND STOCKPOTS; WITHOUT DEDICATED STORAGE, THESE PIECES WILL CLUTTER YOUR COUNTER—OR YOUR GARAGE.

Amid the modern luxury of a professionally equipped kitchen, an accent of rustic antique charm: a two-toned green coffeepot, found at a charming brocante shop in France's Loire Valley.

CULINARY LUXURY

Food is inherently sensuous: luscious red berries, earthy wild mushrooms, intoxicating fragrant herbs. Raw or elaborately prepared, humble or fancy, food is a siren for our senses, constantly amazing us with its range of colors, textures, smells, and, of course, tastes.

In this kitchen, the rich details enhance food's naturally luxurious appeal. In one corner, inviting, fresh golden-hued Bosc pears are posed before an oil painting depicting the same fruit. The arrangement of fresh pears in a gold-painted pedestal bowl before the painting framed in a gold-leaf frame (as is the mirror behind it) allows each enchanting touch to play off one another. The whole scene is further augmented by the copper-backed candleholder and the brass of the drawer pulls and the chandelier. And the tableau is completed with a rich table setting that includes estate silver and incredibly soft napkins. The result is warm and enticing: from this kitchen, you can expect a true feast for all the senses.

SMART TIP ALTHOUGH THESE NAPKINS LOOK LUXURIOUS (AND EXPENSIVE), THEY WERE ACTUALLY SEWN QUICKLY AND EASILY FROM REMNANTS LEFT FROM VARIOUS OTHER PROJECTS. YOU NEVER KNOW WHEN FABRIC SCRAPS MIGHT COME IN HANDY.

LEFT: A profusion of gold tones creates an unmistakably opulent scene. ABOVE: These silver spoons, picked up for a song at an estate sale (they were not in a full set), needed nothing more than elbow grease and the right occasion to regain their lost glory.

WINE LOVER'S PARADISE

Beyond the basic needs, a kitchen can cater to specific whims: a pizza fanatic can install a small pizza oven, a pastry expert can put in a baker's rack and a counter space devoted to rolling dough. In this kitchen, a dedicated oenophile has left his mark: a temperature- and humidity-controlled wine cabinet in which to age those great wines to their peak.

When choosing a new home or redecorating an old one, take a moment to consider your real-life requirements before indulging your decorating fantasies. This is as important in the kitchen as anywhere else. If it's been years since you saw the inside of your oven and the Chinese take-out restaurant knows your children's middle names, you don't need a professional stove; if your daily fare emerges from the microwave, it wouldn't make sense to shove that appliance on top of the refrigerator.

SMART TIP **TAKE THE TIME TO ORGANIZE YOUR KITCHEN TOOLS WHERE YOU WILL BE ABLE TO FIND THEM: THE FEW MINUTES INVESTED WILL BE RECAPTURED THE FIRST TIME YOU *DON'T* HAVE TO SPEND A HALF HOUR LOOKING FOR THE CORKSCREW.**

A bartender's delight: wineglasses hang from a rack, while the fine crystal and specialty glasses are stored in the cabinets above.

STAGES 1-2-3

STAGE 1 **After paying the contractor for the cabinets, you'll want to stick to the basics—albeit ones that you'll keep for a long time: a contemporary farmhouse table with bow-backed Windsor chairs.**

STAGE 2 **A rug always helps define a seating area and organize a room: here, a simple cotton rug provides a lot of bang for the buck.**

STAGE 3 **Apply some finishing touches: a wrought-iron chandelier to replace the outdated track lighting, and seat cushions to create a bit more comfort and color. A smooth, easy transition from stage 1 to stage 3.**

THE BEDROOM

The bedroom is the place for sleep and, of course, dreams—and not only the dreams of that perfect vacation or a lucrative investment, but your decorating dreams as well. This most personal, most intimate room is also the most private room—the room where you can focus on your own tastes and desires. So here's where to take some risks, to indulge your design fantasies, to create a space that is just for you.

Of course, comfort must be a priority—a supportive mattress, soft sheets, a nightstand for necessities, enough window coverings to allow for a Sunday-morning sleep-in. But beyond these basic requirements, the privacy of the bedroom is an invitation to creativity: buy that impractical piece of furniture from the flea market; take home that beloved rug even though you can't see it working in your living room. In the bedroom, whatever makes you happy and comfortable is welcome.

ROMANESQUE MURAL PAINTING
MARILYN MONROE

SMART TIP FRAMED ARTWORK DOESN'T NEED TO BE HUNG TO BE APPRECIATED: LEAVING IT ON TOP OF MANTELS OR FURNITURE, OR EVEN ON THE FLOOR IF IT'S LARGE ENOUGH, PROJECTS A RELAXED FEEL AND IS INFINITELY FLEXIBLE, ALLOWING YOU TO REPLACE, REARRANGE, AND REFOCUS AT WILL.

This beautiful—and very private—guest room was fashioned out of an old carriage house. The unconventional arrangement of furniture combined with the striking whitewashed stone walls make this a truly unique refuge.

FOUR-POSTER FANTASY

This Zen-like bedroom is a thoroughly attainable fantasy of calm, order, and rest—a perfect refuge. While ornate four-poster beds are often associated with an opulent, heavily draped look (think of a Versailles boudoir), the clean, unornamented lines of this piece set a tone that's anything but cluttered and overdone.

The serene statement made with the design of the bed is carried through in the details. Instead of a fussy canopy in a bold color, this organdy one is both tailored and light, simply constructed like a roll-up shade. The muted greens and yellows of the duvet cover are echoed in the colors of the wall, ceiling, and base molding, and are nicely complemented by the soft chenille rug. And the whole room is dominated by the warm, honeyed tones of natural oak-plank floors. But this light palette is tied together with the touches of dark brown: not only in the chair, bed, bench, and table, but also in the picture frames and in the structure of the lampshade.

SMART TIP A FOUR-POSTER BED CAN HAVE MANY DIFFERENT LOOKS—WITH A VERY SIMPLE CHANGE OF CANOPY, YOU CAN CREATE AN ENTIRELY NEW FEELING. KEEP A FEW ON HAND FOR SEASONAL REDECORATING, OR JUST FOR A WHIM.

ABOVE: Besides its utilitarian roles, a bench at the foot of the bed goes a long way to rounding out the decor. RIGHT: A serene palette is the perfect antidote to stress and hurry—and the perfect invitation to lie down, shut your eyes, and drift off.

SOUTHERN COMFORT

The charm of the old South is neatly captured in this small but comfortable and refined bedroom. Central to the Southern charm is the plantation-style four-poster bed, whose ornate, luxurious woodwork is in direct contrast to the Eastern-influenced simplicity of the bed on the previous pages. The substantial hand-turned rope posts feature intricate pineapples, the symbol of hospitality, conveying both strength and grace.

This bed's canopy and the curtains are of a rough linen, which subtly evokes the Southern sense of luxury in proximity to the natural products of the farm. And the visible, quickly knotted ties reinforce the combination of casual and formal that typifies Southern decorating.

Another cornerstone of the room is the handsome armoire, which offers valuable, flexible storage. It can hide that most essential modern accessory, the television, in a cloak of antebellum style; it's also the perfect repository for quilts, linens, and spare pillows, or can be outfitted as a closet.

SMART TIP CREATE A SENSE OF WHIMSY AND DRAMA IN THE BEDROOM BY PLACING THE BED ON THE DIAGONAL, NOT AGAINST ANY WALLS—THERE'S NO DOUBT WHERE THE CENTER OF THIS STAGE IS.

The bed's materials are echoed in the lamp's—the scheme doesn't look forced because of the two pieces' markedly different scales.

WHITE MAGIC

This little nook in a country cottage in the mountains of North Carolina, with its pretty garden view, is the perfect spot for morning coffee, to catch up on reading, or just to daydream. The overwhelming sense of calm is created with a profusion of crisp, clean whites: versatile and beautiful, white's elegance is hard to beat.

Here, white comes in many textures and subtle variations. The different-size pillows are covered in matelassé, eyelet, and cotton duck. The walls, window frames, and breakfast tray are wood; the cup is ceramic, the napkin linen, and the tulip is soft and delicate. But because of the wonderful view and the ever-changing shadows and highlights created by natural light, this monochromatic palette is the complete opposite of plain.

SMART TIP WITH A CUT-TO-ORDER FOAM CUSHION AND SOME IMAGINATION, A DEEP WINDOWSILL CAN EASILY BECOME A WINDOW SEAT. NOT ONLY ROMANTIC AND COMFORTABLE, WINDOW SEATS ARE ALSO GREAT SPACE SAVERS—ESSENTIALLY, FURNITURE BUILT INTO THE WALL, CREATING SOMETHING USEFUL AND BEAUTIFUL WITHOUT TAKING UP ROOM.

When a simple cup of coffee becomes a magical breakfast, you know you've created a special spot.

SMART TIP ARMOIRES ARE BIG PIECES OF FURNITURE THAT CAN MAKE A SMALL ROOM LOOK CRAMPED. BUT THAT PROBLEM IS SOLVED WITH THIS GLASS FRONT AND MIRRORED BACK, PROVIDING A VIEW OF THE BRIGHT LINENS AS WELL AS CREATING DEPTH.

This plantation-style bedroom is injected with the romance of exotic travel by the inclusion of antique suitcases. Flowers planted in a ceramic urn create a dramatic focal point.

Candles, flowers, and fresh fruit are easy, inexpensive additions to make the bedroom elegant and romantic.

SMART TIP NOT ONLY DOES THIS FREESTANDING MIRROR ADD DRAMA AND A SENSE OF DEPTH, BUT IT ALSO PROVIDES STORAGE OPPORTUNITIES, FILLS IN THE OTHERWISE WASTED SPACE OF THIS CORNER, AND CREATES A ROUNDED EDGE THAT'S MORE HARMONIOUS THAN A NINETY-DEGREE ANGLE.

The rich profusion of pillows, the antique-looking bed linens, the lovely warmth of the colors, and the dramatic freestanding corner mirror together lend a decidedly Victorian elegance to this well-appointed bedroom.

ISLAND TIME

Some like it cool. But some like it hot. A profusion of sedate whites and calm pastels is not for the owner of this room, so she covered the walls in this very strong lime green and dressed the bed in bright linens. But the strength of these colors is balanced by the stately dark furniture and the wood floor, and the result is dramatic and vibrant without being overpowering.

Beyond the wall color, a number of touches create a truly tropical feel: leaving the wood bare suggests the need for a cooling touch on your feet to offset the heat, as the antique fan suggests the need for a breeze; and the graceful curves of the sleigh bed are enhanced by reeding on the headboard and footboard, a tropical texture reminiscent of the woven cane bench that's echoed in the materials of the vintage suitcases.

It's the rare bedroom indeed that boasts a chandelier, and this one makes a singular design statement. Although typically found over the dining room table, there's absolutely no reason why a chandelier can't provide touches of elegance, romance, and drama to the bedroom.

SMART TIP DON'T NEGLECT SEATING IN THE BEDROOM—A PERCH TO PUT ON YOUR SHOES, AT THE VERY LEAST. EVEN THE SMALLEST BEDROOMS CAN USUALLY ACCOMMODATE A BENCH AT THE FOOT OF THE BED OR A SIDE CHAIR IN AN OTHERWISE EMPTY SPACE.

ABOVE: All plaids are not created equal. This tropical scheme is anything but the clubby style of the typical Scottish plaid. RIGHT: The furniture is arranged to enjoy the wonderful light, but not to have it streaming into the sleeper's eyes at dawn.

Sherbet hues are luscious and refreshing, and are natural choices for a colorful bedroom. Here, the tranquility of cool mint walls is balanced by the sunny lemon tones, and both colors are echoed in the Fauve-style prints on the mantel. White is the unifying element, accenting the strong architectural features—the doors, mantel, and cornices.

The furniture, like the color scheme, is light and casual, with warmth imparted by the natural finish of the maple. The playful curves of these pieces balance the formality of the architecture. An even more casual touch is the stack of coffee-table books that creates a makeshift mini end table for a bowl of fruit. And in counterpoint to the classical nature of this room's structural details are a couple of thoroughly contemporary touches: the recessed lighting and the halogen reading lamp. The result is a remarkable juxtaposition of old and new, vibrant and soothing.

SMART TIP DON'T BE AFRAID TO LIBERATE THE BED FROM ITS TRADITIONAL POSITION AGAINST THE WALL. SET IN THE CENTER OF THE ROOM AND FILLED WITH A PLUMP COMFORTER AND PLUSH PILLOWS, THIS BED CREATES AN INVITING ISLAND OF REPOSE.

Balancing warm hues with cool ones, and formal architectural elements with casual furniture lines, creates a unique room.

Warm, golden hues are balanced by the strong lines of dark furniture to create an embracing, elegant, and uncluttered bedroom.

The interesting horizontal lines of the wall planks are reiterated by the slats of the canopy and window shutters.

PLEASING PASTELS

If you're blessed with an old house that boasts good bones, you have many and varied decorating options—including the option to let the charms of the house itself drive the decor. Here, the wonderful old wide-planked wooden floors and the restrained beauty of the small fireplace dominate the room. Left uncovered, the floors are finished with traditional wax rather than modern polyurethane; wax imparts less of a tint to the natural wood, and the finish is flat rather than glossy, more appropriate for creating a period atmosphere—albeit requiring more effort to maintain (wax must be reapplied at least a few times per year, depending on traffic).

The cool, muted hues of the wall and slipcover prevent a monochromatic look, but the color is more of an accent than a dominating element. Instead, what dominates are the natural woods and the creams that are used for the fireplace and trim as well as the bedding and the objects on the mantel, complemented by the perennial elegance of gold-colored frames. The overall effect is strikingly soothing in its simplicity.

SMART TIP SLIPCOVERS FOR CHAIRS AND SOFAS ARE AN EXCELLENT, RELATIVELY INEXPENSIVE WAY TO PROVIDE SEASONAL VARIATION TO YOUR DECOR—AND ALSO AN EASY WAY TO PREVENT, REMOVE, OR HIDE THE INEVITABLE DIRT AND STAINS.

LEFT: The hallmark of this bedroom is a less-is-more approach that showcases the innate beauty of the old house. ABOVE: Bed linens in different textures and different shades of cream create a relaxed and timeless look.

This sophisticated country bedroom is composed of a symphony of elegant whites: plaster walls, bedcovers in both smooth and waffle weave, and a ceramic jug lamp with white shade, all bound together by dark accents and furniture.

COLOR EXPLOSION

Even if the rest of your house is dominated by cool neutrals or restrained pastels, the bedroom may be the place to unleash your wild color fantasies. The obvious starting point is the bedding, which offers easy, inexpensive, and completely flexible ways to experiment with an infinite variety of color, patterns, and textures.

A color feast was created on this bed by mixing plaids, florals, and solids. Saturated reds dominate and provide a defining color scheme, without which this hodgepodge would look as if each piece was clashing with the others. But the profusion of pillows, sheets, and blankets, nearly all in different patterns, holds together well because of the common color elements—even such touches as the plant and fabric on the end table are picked up in the bedding.

SMART TIP IF YOU WANT TO GO NUTS WITH COLOR FOR YOUR BEDDING, BE SURE TO PROVIDE A NEUTRAL BACKDROP TO AVOID AN OVERLY BUSY LOOK. HERE, THE BOLDNESS OF THE BEDDING IS OFFSET BY THE OFF-WHITE HEADBOARD AND THE WHITE COVERLET; AND THE BRILLIANCE OF THE SHEER RED CURTAINS STANDS OUT NICELY AGAINST THE WHITE.

An explosion of color is particularly appealing with good light, bringing out the details of rich patterns and colors.

MOULIN ROUGE
MOULIN ROUGE
MOULIN ROUGE
LA GOULUE
MOULIN ROUGE
Mercredis

SMART TIP ALTHOUGH USING THE SAME FABRIC IN DIFFERENT PARTS OF A ROOM MAY SEEM EASY, THE RESULT IS ALL TOO OFTEN STAGED-LOOKING. INSTEAD, USE MATCHING OR COMPLEMENTARY COLORS BUT IN DIFFERENT PATTERNS OR TEXTURES, SUCH AS THE WARM REDS AND YELLOWS IN THIS ROOM.

The colors are bold and rich, but the neutral accents prevent the room from oversaturation. ABOVE: Continue a bold color scheme by matching flowers to hues on the walls, art, bedding, or drapes, making nature part of your decor.

SMART TIP ROMAN SHADES, SUMPTUOUS YET MODERN, COME IN A VARIETY OF FABRICS, TEXTURES, AND COLORS AND CAN BRING A CONTEMPORARY TOUCH TO TRADITIONALLY FURNISHED ROOMS.

ABOVE: Well-organized and neat but warm and casual—the perfect bedroom mix. **RIGHT:** The wide stripes of the wallpaper and bedding are picked up in the upholstery of the chair, the ribbon of the shades, and even the strong vertical of the bedside lamp.

LEFT: The warmth of yellows is balanced by soothing dusty miller blues, resulting in an inviting, cheery room that's not overpowering. RIGHT: For a fresh, crisp look, nothing beats the combination of whites and neutrals coupled with restrained blue tones.

LOFT LIVING

If warm colors and an intimate space are your ideal, the downtown chic of a loft isn't for you. But if your goal is a pared-down simplicity that contrasts with your hectic life, the soothing neutrals and spare arrangements of this bedroom may be the perfect decor to lull you to sleep.

Everything in this room reflects a sleek, contemporary style: the clean lines of the furniture and the simple, machine-age elegance of the hardware. But the cool neutrals of the upholstery are offset by the abundance of pillows and the layers of bedding.

An often overlooked bonus of this spare elegance is economy: with limited pieces and a carefully edited number of accents, decorating this beautiful room is a quick, relatively inexpensive affair. So if you're just starting out with very few furnishings, this decor—which sacrifices absolutely nothing in terms of flair—may be a wise and stylish choice.

SMART TIP **IF YOU'RE GOING TO LIMIT YOUR WALL DECORATIONS, CONSIDER CHOOSING A PIECE OF FURNITURE THAT'S EITHER HIGH OR HAS SOME VERTICAL ELEMENT, TO PREVENT A SPARSE AND ELEGANT INTENT FROM BECOMING BARE AND UNFINISHED.**

Cool neutrals that are offset by warm woods create a spare and chic bedroom that's still inviting and comfortable.

Gray's Anatomy
Sermon on the Rock
BED
THE BED
BACKYARD BIRDS

SMART TIP TO TAKE ADVANTAGE OF GREAT NATURAL LIGHT AND CREATE A TRULY SPECTACULAR SPACE, CONSIDER THE DRAMA OF WHITEWASHED WOOD FLOORS OR WHITE-PAINTED BRICK WALLS.

LEFT: The monochrome of the white floors and walls is broken up by the natural wood tones and dashes of color on the bed and window. ABOVE: For sheer drama, pair simple, dark furniture against an even more simple white background.

An inviting, layered suite was created out of this large bedroom by installing a screened half-partition, dividing the room into a comfortable bed space and an elegant dressing area, all tied together with a unified palette and style.

STAGES 1-2-3

STAGE 1 **Start with the most important, defining feature of the bedroom—the bed, of course—coupled with an invaluable bedside table. To round out an otherwise sparsely decorated room, add a plant and artwork.**

STAGE 2 **An armoire provides definition to the room, as well as valuable storage space, and is a flexible piece of furniture that can evolve with your needs.**

STAGE 3 **A traditional mirror-topped dresser completes the furniture needs of this room, and a paint job, a rug, and some new art complete the tableau.**

THE KIDS' ROOM

Here's a great room in which to indulge some fantasies—particularly if you can remember what you wanted *your* room to look like when you were young. But the kids' room is, of course, for the kids—and sooner or later, they will want to leave their own imprint. So it's important to be flexible, to let the room evolve as your children grow and as their tasks and hobbies and needs evolve.

It's also important to talk to your children about what they want and need out of their rooms—not necessarily to indulge their every passing fancy, but to ensure that their actual requirements are met. Don't underestimate their sophistication or their ability to communicate, and you'll find a treasure trove of practical advice. While you're bound to hear some far-fetched schemes for installing a basketball court or the cockpit of a spaceship, you'll also learn some fascinating things about their day-to-day lives.

ON THE WILD SIDE

If there's one place you can go absolutely wild with colors and patterns, it's in your child's room—especially if your child is on the wild side. In this room, the mix-and-match ethic is encapsulated by the bed: the duvet's print is composed of bright, child-like designs; the yellow plaid sheets and pillowcase don't match the different plaid of the bed skirt or the floral of the other pillowcases, not to mention the duvet. And this sense of play permeates every detail, from the repetition of a favorite fabric (in the curtain, pillowcases, even covering the boxes on the floor) to the proud display of toys.

In an adult's room, this type of treatment would probably be a little *too* wild. But in a child's room, the combination looks joyful and fun. And no matter how restrained or elegant the rest of your home, joyful and fun are good ideals for this room.

SMART TIP CHILDREN ARE INVETERATE COLLECTORS, AND THEY SHOULD BE ALLOWED EASY ACCESS TO WHATEVER ENDS UP BEING THEIR FAVORITE COLLECTION. ALTHOUGH IT'S IMPORTANT TO IMPOSE SOME ORDER, IT'S ALSO IMPORTANT TO ALLOW YOUR CHILD TO EXPLORE HER CREATIVITY AND HAVE FUN WITH HER BELONGINGS.

A profusion of colors, patterns, and textures ensures that this room reflects all the wonder and excitement of its resident.

SUGAR AND SPICE

It's hard not to succumb to the charms of a little girl's room. As much as we may want to resist a totally feminine room filled with pink and frills, a little girlishness can melt our hearts without being cloying.

Just because you need to achieve the right scale (and safety measures) doesn't mean you must limit yourself to specially constructed children's furniture. On the left, a painted daybed with scrolled arms is the perfect size for a child, but is not an "official" child's bed. And the two-drawer Provençal-style table makes a perfect nightstand and storage space. But when this girl gets older and wants to redecorate, this table will be able to find an equally appropriate home elsewhere in the house.

The sophisticated country air of the room on the right is perfect for a preteen. The subtle color scheme is just sweet enough but doesn't go too far, and the frilly touches are elegant without being overdone. The canopied bed creates a private refuge in which to ponder the unimaginable challenges of being young.

SMART TIP BE SURE TO USE MATS BENEATH RUGS IN CHILDREN'S ROOMS (IF NOT THE WHOLE HOUSE), TO PREVENT SLIPS, FALLS, AND INJURIES—CHILDREN WILL GET INTO ENOUGH TROUBLE WITHOUT ADDING THE UNNECESSARY HAZARD OF UNSTABLE FOOTING.

An elegant, grown-up-looking bed goes a long way toward giving these girls' rooms a sense of sophistication and responsibility.

SEARCHING FOR STORAGE

Ask any parent about the most essential element of a child's room, and the consensus is clear: you can never have too much storage space. Children squirrel away everything, from fast-food giveaways and birthday cards to old stuffed animals and broken toys. And then, of course, there are the piles of papers, books, and artwork that seem to grow a foot each night, not to mention the detritus of the latest science project.

What can you do with all this mess? Rather than make midnight raids to winnow out what you consider unnecessary—and run the inevitable risk of hearing a tear-filled "But I *needed* that"—reconcile yourself to the situation. And one of the first things to consider is shelving. Toys, books, trophies, dolls—you name it and it can find a home on a set of open shelves. Add a few drawers and a desk with a slide-out keyboard tray, and voilà: the explosion of belongings is off the floor and organized.

SMART TIP FICKLE TASTES IN ARTWORK ARE INEVITABLE. TAPE WILL CREATE A PROFUSION OF RIPPED PAINT OR WALLPAPER; NAILS AND PUSHPINS WILL POCKMARK THE WALLS OR FILL THEM WITH HOLES. SO THINK ABOUT INSTALLING AT LEAST ONE BULLETIN BOARD.

Although not the most orderly shelves in your home, children's bookcases are essential to hold their ever-changing collections.

SMART TIP ALLOW YOUR CHILD INTO THE DESIGN PROCESS BY LETTING HER CHOOSE HER OWN PAINT COLORS. THIS LITTLE GIRL LOVES BEING SURROUNDED BY THE MEADOW GREEN AND SKY BLUE, ALTHOUGH SHE INSISTED THAT THE SKY BE ON THE BOTTOM AND THE MEADOW ON THE TOP. THESE STRONG COLORS ARE TIED TOGETHER WITH THE WHITE TRIM, AND THE RESULT IS ANYTHING BUT JARRING.

SWEET DREAMS

Lull your baby into a gentle sleep in this lovely old-world nursery. The colors are warm and muted in rich vanillas; the floors are naturally finished with a soft shine. The braided rug helps define the natural focal point: the traditional crib.

What makes this room perfect is that everything is arranged for a low eye level: the half-height bookshelves, the small French armoire, and even the low-hung picture are all in keeping with the height of a toddler. While this may make you feel like Gulliver, remember that the point of this room is to make your child comfortable.

Nevertheless, your needs as a parent must be met. Those needs will include access to more sheets, blankets, towels, and diapers than you can possibly imagine—and you'll want to have them close at hand, not down the hall on an upper shelf of the linen closet. A small-scale armoire is perfect: with easy access, choices at a glance, and ample room.

SMART TIP **IN THE NURSERY, EXPECT THE UNEXPECTED, INCLUDING RAPIDLY CHANGING NEEDS FOR FURNISHINGS AND SUPPLIES. BE SURE TO BUDGET MONEY (AND TIME) FOR SOME RECONSIDERATIONS.**

LEFT: The shape and style of the armoire are elegant, but a playful touch is provided by the hangers. TOP: The only adult-scale furniture is the one piece for an adult—the rocking chair. ABOVE: A classic linen choice for nurseries is candy striping.

ZACK

SMART TIP **INFANCY IS VERY SHORT. SO A SAFER, LESS LABOR-INTENSIVE OPTION THAN AN OVER-THE-TOP NURSERY IS TO USE SMALL ACCENTS RATHER THAN LARGE-SCALE INVESTMENTS.**

LEFT: In this tiny room without a closet, the tall chest of drawers provides all the necessary storage space. ABOVE: Although there's nothing cutesy about this room and the color scheme is far from pastel, it's still without a doubt a nursery.

THE BATHROOM

Think of it as the ultimate hideaway: close the doors and leave the world on the other side. The bathroom is the one place where you can expect total peace and privacy—and in this ever more wired, networked, connected universe, time to yourself might be the most valuable of all commodities.

ncreasingly, people are recognizing that the true hallmark of luxury is the perfectly appointed bathroom. New home building has seen a dramatic rise in the size and priority devoted to bathrooms, especially to master baths, some of which rival bedrooms in scale and decorating. But scale and expense do not necessarily add up to style, and neither may be necessary to achieve your personal vision of luxury. Whether your vision is an outdoor shower in Bali or a sophisticated marble bath in a European grand hotel, little touches can go a long way. New wallpaper, different window treatments, a new set of towels, or simply a bowl of soaps can work wonders.

THE GREENHOUSE BATH

All too often, achieving total privacy in the bathroom means blocking out any views in—and, hence, any views out. But if you're lucky enough to have a bath's window that faces nothing but your private property, seize the opportunity to let the outdoors in.

Here, this huge paned window looks out onto a patch of rocky forest, giving the bath a greenhouse look. Whether by sunlight or moonlight, nature is part of the experience of bathing. But the tufted chair and matching cushions, not typical elements of a bathroom, impart an air of grandeur.

SMART TIP ANY BATHROOM CAN BENEFIT FROM HANGING AT LEAST ONE PIECE OF ART, A MUCH-OVERLOOKED NECESSITY FOR NEARLY ANY ROOM. JUST A SIMPLE PRINT, A FAMILY PHOTOGRAPH, OR A SMALL DRAWING CAN MAKE ALL THE DIFFERENCE, ESPECIALLY CONSIDERING HOW LITTLE WALL SPACE MOST BATHROOMS BOAST. BUT BEWARE THE HIGH HUMIDITY OF BATHROOMS, NOT TO MENTION THE OCCASIONAL SPLASH—THEY CAN DO GREAT DAMAGE TO ORIGINAL PIECES OF ART.

Since the Romans, bathers have recognized the unequaled beauty and practicality of marble: here, cream-colored travertine.

SMART TIP SMALL PIECES OF OCCASIONAL FURNITURE CAN ADD CHARACTER AND STYLE TO A BATH. THIS IS THE PERFECT PLACE FOR THAT EXTRA SIDE TABLE FOUND AT A FLEA MARKET OR THE SMALL CHEST OF DRAWERS THAT DOESN'T EXACTLY FIT IN WITH YOUR OTHER DECORATING SCHEMES.

Even without the other fine decorative touches, the elegant picture molding would make this bathroom distinctive. ABOVE: A clubby, gentlemanlike feel is achieved through the dark wainscoting and bird-motif wallpaper.

BATH ON WHEELS

If you've got space to spare, don't hesitate to bring in some real furniture. The most intriguing bathrooms contain elements of surprise—an antique dresser, a woven rug, even an upholstered chaise longue.

A tall glass curio cabinet stands proudly in the middle of this bath, beckoning through the open French doors. Although the curio cabinet provides practical storage space for sumptuous towels, it would serve equally well holding toiletries or even purely decorative objects. But more important, it's another layer of interest to this impressive room. The slipper chair and glass-topped side table are other unexpected touches, all adding up to a truly unique bath.

But although the unexpected may provide glamour, make sure that you don't ruin your valuables: the bathroom is not the place for a chair upholstered in antique Chinese silk, an original watercolor, a prized antique wooden table, or anything else that could be damaged by water in a typical bathroom.

SMART TIP MAKE SURE BATHROOM FURNITURE IS SUITED TO HIGH HUMIDITY AND WON'T SUFFER FROM A BIT OF WATER. FOR UPHOLSTERY, COTTON IS THE NATURAL CHOICE, AND TEXTURED FABRICS SUCH AS TERRY ARE EASY TO MAINTAIN AND STAIN-RESISTANT.

If you're especially careful, the edge of the tub may be an acceptable place to balance a book or arrange some candles. But for more comfort and safety, add a small table (LEFT) or a built-in step-ledge (RIGHT).

Nickel-plated fixtures, such as this faucet and handheld shower, add classic glamour to any bath.

STAGES 1-2-3

STAGE 1 **This capacious bath is given some personality with a few botanical prints and a small stool to fill in space.**

STAGE 2 **Adding a rug provides warmth, texture, and color, and a small rug that might be lost in a large living room goes a long way in the bathroom.**

STAGE 3 **Filling out the room are a tea cart on wheels, for extra storage and surface area, and a simple rattan bench covered in durable cotton. Just these relatively inexpensive pieces make the difference between a nice bath and a downright luxurious one.**

壽

THE HOME OFFICE

Office/home; work/play; speed/sleep. These days, with dot-coms starting on kitchen tables and on-line auction bidding late into the night, the distinction between home and work is increasingly blurred—and the need for a distinct home office space is increasingly evident.

Working in a T-shirt and jeans with your dog at your feet provides a greater sense of freedom than toiling away at the office. But work is still work, and it comes with an ever-widening array of technological needs and options. Yet despite the profusion of home offices, we don't necessarily have more space. So the challenges are many: to create an organized, efficient, yet interesting space that fits your work habits and needs. Your office space must also reflect your personal style without ruining the decor of the room from which it's carved, or, if you have a dedicated office, a style that's not out of character with the rest of your home. But these challenges are far from insurmountable.

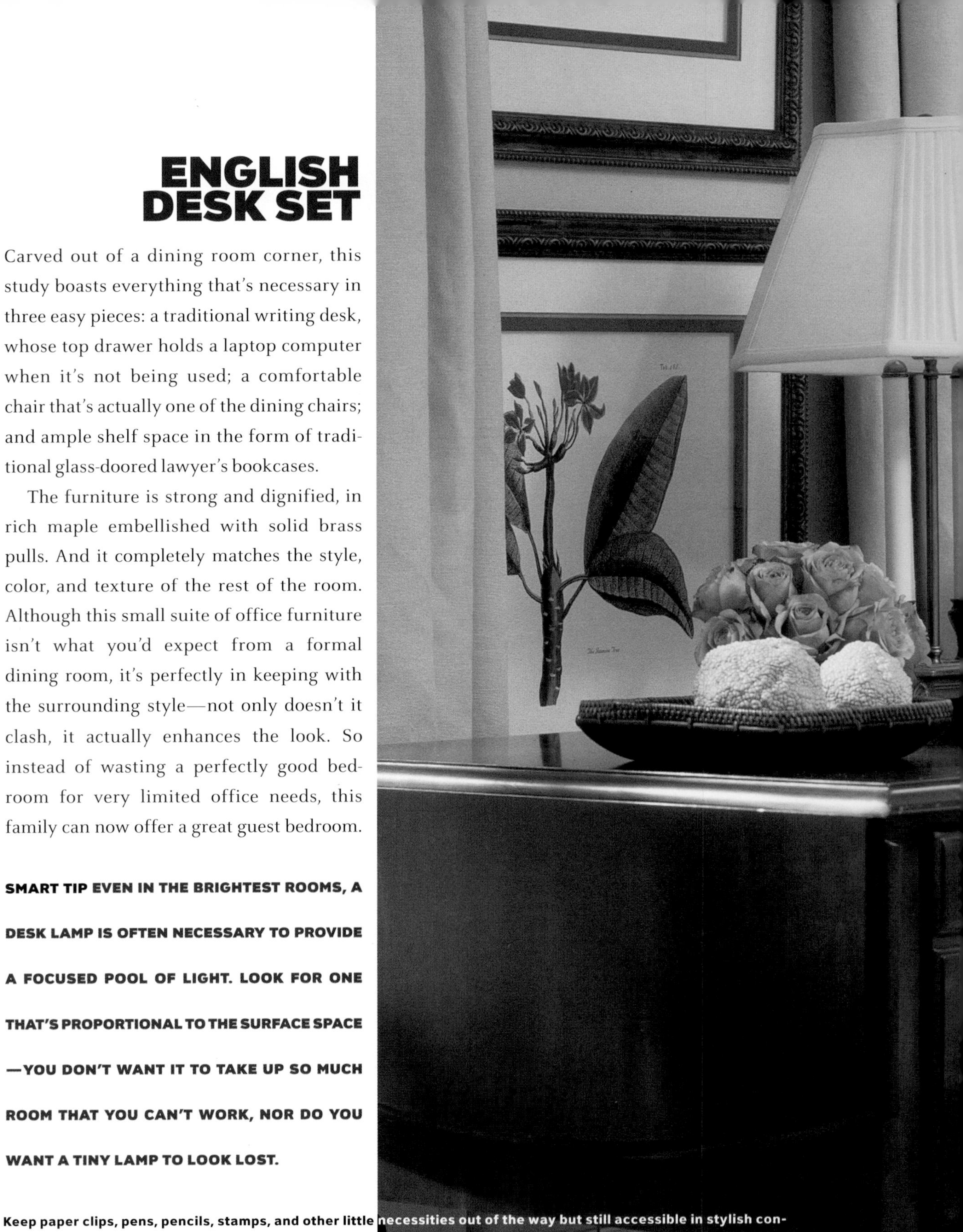

ENGLISH DESK SET

Carved out of a dining room corner, this study boasts everything that's necessary in three easy pieces: a traditional writing desk, whose top drawer holds a laptop computer when it's not being used; a comfortable chair that's actually one of the dining chairs; and ample shelf space in the form of traditional glass-doored lawyer's bookcases.

The furniture is strong and dignified, in rich maple embellished with solid brass pulls. And it completely matches the style, color, and texture of the rest of the room. Although this small suite of office furniture isn't what you'd expect from a formal dining room, it's perfectly in keeping with the surrounding style—not only doesn't it clash, it actually enhances the look. So instead of wasting a perfectly good bedroom for very limited office needs, this family can now offer a great guest bedroom.

SMART TIP EVEN IN THE BRIGHTEST ROOMS, A DESK LAMP IS OFTEN NECESSARY TO PROVIDE A FOCUSED POOL OF LIGHT. LOOK FOR ONE THAT'S PROPORTIONAL TO THE SURFACE SPACE —YOU DON'T WANT IT TO TAKE UP SO MUCH ROOM THAT YOU CAN'T WORK, NOR DO YOU WANT A TINY LAMP TO LOOK LOST.

Keep paper clips, pens, pencils, stamps, and other little necessities out of the way but still accessible in stylish containers such as these stackable wooden boxes.

COLOR COLLECTION

SMART TIP JUST BECAUSE IT'S YOUR OFFICE DOESN'T MEAN IT MUST BE ALL WORK AND NO PLAY. ART, PERSONAL PHOTOGRAPHS, AND OTHER NONESSENTIAL ITEMS CAN TURN A NO-NONSENSE PLACE TO TOIL INTO A STYLISH NOOK. AND A VASE OF FLOWERS NEVER HURT ANYONE'S PRODUCTIVITY.

Black-and-white photographs are a classic choice for a sedate yet chic office. When wall space is at a premium, don't be afraid to prop art on surfaces, such as on the desk at left, or even to hang frames from bookshelves.

SMART TIP IN ANY OFFICE, WHETHER AT HOME OR IN A CORPORATE HIGH-RISE, ORGANIZATION IS ESSENTIAL. IF YOU CAN'T FIND YOUR FILES, NOTES, STATIONERY, AND OTHER NECESSITIES WHEN YOU NEED THEM, THEN YOU'RE NOT DOING YOURSELF ANY GOOD. IN THIS SPARE, ELEGANT OFFICE, EVERYTHING IS IN ITS PLACE—AND CAN BE FOUND WITH THE SIMPLE PULL OF A DRAWER.

ABOVE: If you allow yourself more shelf space than you actually need, you can create a clean, spare look that focuses attention on your beautiful objects. If these shelves were crammed full, the well-chosen pieces would be lost.

Henry Gray F.R.S.
Gray's Anatomy
THE LIMITS OF ART
MOVING PICTURES
MAILER
PETER MANSO
LEGENDS OF THE WORLD
Robert James Waller
Serpent on the Rock
ANSEL ADAMS
COMMUNICATION ARTS
ELMORE LEONARD

UNDER THE EAVES

If your home-office requirements are limited to a place to store some files and a few books, you may not need to impose these items on a dining or living room. Take a few moments to look around your house for out-of-the-way, unused spaces that might fit to a tee.

In this third-floor attic family room, the wall under the eaves was home to nothing more than a poster. Three maple bookcases in graduated heights are a perfect match for the space, and a rolling file box rounds out this family's office requirements.

With a little searching and creativity, similar spaces can be found in all but the most crowded homes: a wall and corner in a large bedroom or dining room, a section of the foyer, or even in the often-neglected hallway between many a kitchen and dining room—all places that might accommodate an arrangement such as this, creating valuable office space from what might otherwise be wasted space.

SMART TIP WHEN ARRANGING BOOKS, PAPERS, AND OTHER OBJECTS ON SHELVES, TRY TO BALANCE THE CONTENT OF THE SHELVES, MIXING DIFFERENT TYPES OF ITEMS ON THE SAME SHELF. THIS PROVIDES EACH SHELF WITH MORE DISTINCTION THAN IF A NUMBER OF SIMILAR ITEMS WERE PLACED TOGETHER.

The warm hues of the shelves, floor, and walls make this third-floor nook anything but a cobweb- and clutter-filled attic.

STAGES 1-2-3

STAGE 1 The basic work unit—shelves with a computer desk and keyboard tray—serves most purposes of this textile designer. Files are kept in handy file boxes.

STAGE 2 To accommodate expanding files and other material, the work unit is augmented with a matching second unit and a wicker basket for more files. And the dining chair is traded in for a proper office chair that swivels.

STAGE 3 Finally, another bookcase (against the far wall) is added to accommodate the burgeoning records of a successful business, and a small sofa provides seating for guests.

SUMMER
1993
POEMS six
ARCHITECTURAL

THE OUTDOOR ROOM

One of the largest, most luxurious, most interesting rooms in your home may turn out to be not a room at all—the outdoors. While some people look at a backyard and have visions of a rigidly organized formal garden or a perfectly level clay tennis court (or, conversely, an endless source of weed-fighting frustration), others see something quite different: an opportunity to create a unique, supremely comfortable area to entertain friends, spend time with family, or simply unwind after the rigors of a workday.

Think of your yard as an extension of your home. Apply the same sense of style and taste to your outdoor area. Don't limit your outdoor room strictly to "patio" furniture. And as soon as the weather turns warm, throw open the doors and watch your living space expand exponentially. Suddenly, you can relax, dine, entertain, or even sleep under the sun and moon and stars, surrounded by lush grass, fragrant flowers, and fresh air.

MANGER À LA JARDIN

Whether it's a casual brunch under blue skies, a backyard barbecue for the Fourth of July, or a formal dinner under a blanket of stars, it's hard to beat the romance of an outdoor meal. And it's a snap to decorate while taking advantage of the natural elements.

Start with your location. If you're planning a midday meal in the dog days of August, you'll want to locate yourself in the shade and, hopefully, a breeze. Any spot next to water will be cooler; when it's hot out, water is cooler than the air, and the wind blowing across the water will be chilled. But in spring and fall, if the strength of the sun is welcome, take advantage of the warming sunshine and plop down in the brightest spot possible.

If the sun will be setting during your meal, site your table in a spot with the best view. (Also have plenty of mosquito repellant on hand.) For a postsunset meal, make sure that you have an unobstructed view of the heavens above—there are no better candles for a candlelight dinner than the constellations.

SMART TIP IF YOU'RE SERVING DINNER AT DUSK, TAKE CARE WITH THE SEATING. ALTHOUGH YOU'LL WANT TO OFFER A VIEW OF THE SUNSET, TRY NOT TO HAVE ANYONE FACING *DIRECTLY* INTO THE SUN.

ABOVE: A perfect garden lunch is set in the midst of the flowering garden, whose lushness is reinforced by the mixed bouquet on the table. RIGHT: Create the unexpected by bringing indoor elements to the outdoors, such as this wrought-iron chandelier.

This is truly splendor in the grass—a handsome chair, a good book, and the scent of flowers in bloom.

PALATIAL PATIOS

Halfway between interior and decidedly exterior, the patio, deck, or porch is the most natural and convenient spot for an outdoor room, offering the best of both worlds. The ground is level, access to the inside is easy, electricity is possible, and even a covering of some sort may be on hand to protect from unexpected rains or undesirable heat. But you still have the views, gentle breezes, and the all-too-rare feeling of breathing fresh air.

The shelter provided by these spaces also creates an opportunity to get creative with your furnishings. Here, a British classic sideboard has broken free from the confines of the dining room and introduces a welcome surprise: a touch of formality to offset the casual environment.

A few other formal touches complete the scene: candlesticks with tapers, a silver teapot, cloth napkins, elegant china and flatware. Although this is clearly a relaxed luncheon, the setting also lets the guests know that they're important enough to take some trouble for. And that, after all, is the essence of entertaining.

SMART TIP THE KEY TO CREATING SPECIAL SPACES IS TO INTRODUCE THE UNEXPECTED. THESE CREATIVE TOUCHES ARE WHAT YOUR GUESTS WILL MOST CLEARLY REMEMBER. AND IN NO ROOM IS THIS MORE EASILY ACHIEVED THAN THE OUTDOOR ROOM.

The lushness of the garden is reflected in the profusion of plantings and the variety of cut flowers on this patio—and, of course, in the delicious and colorful lunch on the table.

MARGINS

SMART TIP EVEN IF YOUR BEACH HOUSE IS BLESSED WITH AN EXPANSIVE DECK, YOU'LL WANT TO BRING LUNCH OUT OF THE DIRECT SUN DURING THE HEAT OF THE SUMMER. A NICE COMPROMISE IS TO SET YOUR TABLE JUST INSIDE THE DOOR, ADMITTING BREEZE AND LIGHT BUT PROVIDING MUCH-NEEDED SHADE.

Although most outdoor furniture is modeled on traditional garden furniture, there's no reason why you can't go for a sleek, thoroughly contemporary look, as with these futuristic-looking pieces.

WATERSIDE WEEKENDS

Whether it's a pool, creek, river, lake, or ocean, it's hard to match the relaxed luxury and sheer fun of the water. If you're lucky enough to have a house that boasts waterfront views or a pool, it goes without saying that you'll want to take full advantage of this unparalleled resource.

Of course, the water itself isn't something you're going to decorate. But that doesn't mean the *waterside* should be left to its own natural devices. To get the most out of your water access, you'll want to carefully choose and arrange a few pieces of furniture for maximum benefit.

A dock, whose utilitarian purpose is to provide access to a boat, also provides wonderful opportunities to create unexpected living spaces. With some comfortable seating and an elegant railing, this becomes the perfect place to relax with your favorite book, catch up on some work, or simply take a nap. Weather permitting, such outdoor spaces are often used much more than indoor ones; shouldn't they be decorated accordingly?

SMART TIP IF YOU ARE GOING TO LEAVE CUSHIONS OUTSIDE, BE SURE TO FIND THOSE THAT HAVE UV PROTECTION (TO RESIST FADING), STAIN PROTECTION, AND DO NOT RETAIN WATER (FOR QUICK DRYING).

ABOVE: The views and breezes make this beautiful dock a perfect place for unwinding. RIGHT: The classic choice for poolside relaxation is the adjustable, upholstered chaise longue.

SMART TIP ALL TOO OFTEN, DECK FURNITURE IS MADE OF THE SAME WOOD WITH THE SAME FINISH AS THE DECK, WHICH CAN LOOK DRABLY MONOCHROMATIC. FOR A MORE APPEALING, RICH LOOK, CHOOSE FURNITURE IN A CONTRASTING COLOR, TEXTURE, OR FINISH. OR ADD CONTRASTING ACCENTS, SUCH AS PLANTERS, UPHOLSTERY, OR EVEN A STURDY VASE.

Just beyond the kitchen's sliding glass door, this poolside deck boasts a perfect (and convenient) spot for lunch. RIGHT: The sleek, modern shape of this slatted chaise provides a striking counterpoint to the view beyond.

ETHAN ALLEN DIRECTORY

UNITED STATES

ALABAMA

Birmingham
Ethan Allen Home Interiors
1069 Montgomery Highway

Dothan
Ethan Allen Home Interiors
3282 Montgomery Highway

Huntsville
Ethan Allen Home Interiors
3017 South Memorial Parkway

Mobile
Ethan Allen Home Interiors
4023 Airport Boulevard

Montgomery
Ethan Allen Home Interiors
3300 Eastern Boulevard

ARIZONA

Glendale
Ethan Allen Home Interiors
7760 West Bell Road

Mesa
Ethan Allen Home Interiors
1710 South Alma School Road

Phoenix
Ethan Allen Home Interiors
5301 North 16th Street

Scottsdale
Ethan Allen Home Interiors
11201 North Scottsdale Road

Tucson
Ethan Allen Home Interiors
5621 North Oracle Road

CALIFORNIA

Artesia
Ethan Allen Home Interiors
11720 East South Street

Concord
Ethan Allen Home Interiors
2080 Diamond Boulevard

Costa Mesa
Ethan Allen Home Interiors
1835 Newport Boulevard
Suite 139

Fairfield
Ethan Allen Home Interiors
5111 Business Center Drive

Fresno
Ethan Allen Home Interiors
3011 East Shields Avenue

Glendale
Ethan Allen Home Interiors
300 North Brand Boulevard

Lake Forest
Ethan Allen Home Interiors
23222 Lake Center Drive

La Mesa
Ethan Allen Home Interiors
8185 Fletcher Parkway

Mill Valley
Ethan Allen Home Interiors
1060 Redwood Highway

Montclair
Ethan Allen Home Interiors
5001 South Plaza Lane

Mountain View
Ethan Allen Home Interiors
861 East El Camino Real

Newark
Ethan Allen Home Interiors
5763 Stevenson Boulevard

Northridge
Ethan Allen Home Interiors
8750 Tampa Avenue

Pasadena
Ethan Allen Home Interiors
445 North Rosemead
Boulevard

Pleasanton
Ethan Allen Home Interiors
4230 Rosewood Drive

Redding
Ethan Allen Home Interiors
307 Park Marina Circle

Sacramento
Ethan Allen Home Interiors
525 Fulton Avenue

Ethan Allen Home Interiors
5130 Madison Avenue

San Bernardino
Ethan Allen Home Interiors
1363 South E Street

San Diego
Ethan Allen Home Interiors
7341 Clairemont Mesa
Boulevard

San Jose
Ethan Allen Home Interiors
2500 Fontaine Road

San Marcos
Ethan Allen Home Interiors
1040 Los Vallecitos Boulevard

San Mateo
Ethan Allen Home Interiors
3020 Bridgepointe Parkway

Santa Ana
Ethan Allen Home Interiors
2101 North Tustin Avenue

Santa Rosa
Ethan Allen Home Interiors
2503 Cleveland Avenue

Saratoga
Ethan Allen Home Interiors
5285 Prospect Road

Thousand Oaks
Ethan Allen Home Interiors
111 South Westlake Boulevard
Suite 103

Torrance
Ethan Allen Home Interiors
2700 West Sepulveda
Boulevard

Ventura
Ethan Allen Home Interiors
3970 East Main Street

West Los Angeles
Ethan Allen Home Interiors
11419 Santa Monica Boulevard

Whittier
Ethan Allen Home Interiors
16269 East Whittier Boulevard

COLORADO

Aurora
Ethan Allen Home Interiors
1690 South Chambers Road

Colorado Springs
Ethan Allen Home Interiors
7298 North Academy
Boulevard

Fort Collins
Ethan Allen Home Interiors
4636 South Mason Street

Littleton
Ethan Allen Home Interiors
4151 East County Line Road

Westminster
Ethan Allen Home Interiors
8780 West 101st Avenue and
Wadsworth Parkway

CONNECTICUT

Canton
Ethan Allen Home Interiors
135 Albany Turnpike

Clinton
Ethan Allen Home Interiors
2 Killingworth Turnpike

Danbury
Ethan Allen Home Interiors
Ethan Allen Drive

Groton
Ethan Allen Home Interiors
721 Long Hill Road

Manchester
Ethan Allen Home Interiors
49 Hale Road

Milford
Ethan Allen Home Interiors
1620 Boston Post Road

Norwalk
Ethan Allen Home Interiors
556 Main Avenue

Southington
Ethan Allen Home Interiors
228 Queen Street

Stamford
Ethan Allen Home Interiors
2046 West Main Street

DELAWARE

Wilmington
Ethan Allen Home Interiors
4507 Kirkwood Highway

DISTRICT OF COLUMBIA

Washington, D.C.
Ethan Allen Home Interiors
4473 Connecticut Avenue NW

FLORIDA

Altamonte Springs
Ethan Allen Home Interiors
249 West Highway 436
Suite 1033

Boca Raton
Ethan Allen Home Interiors
9200 West Glades Road

Fort Lauderdale
Ethan Allen Home Interiors
2900 North Federal Highway

Fort Myers
Ethan Allen Home Interiors
16240 South Tamiami Trail

Jacksonville
Ethan Allen Home Interiors
7666 Blanding Boulevard

Ethan Allen Home Interiors
10452 Phillips Highway

Lakeland
Ethan Allen Home Interiors
4505 South Florida Avenue

Melbourne
Ethan Allen Home Interiors
2705 North Harbor City
Boulevard

Miami
Ethan Allen Home Interiors
15053 South Dixie Highway

Naples
Ethan Allen Home Interiors
3000 North Tamiami Trail

Orlando
Ethan Allen Home Interiors
9677 South Orange Blossom
Trail

Ormond Beach
Ethan Allen Home Interiors
450 South Yonge Street
U.S. Highway 1

Osprey
Ethan Allen Home Interiors
1200 South Tamiami Trail

Pembroke Pines
Ethan Allen Home Interiors
13680 Pines Boulevard

Pensacola
Ethan Allen Home Interiors
6235 North Davis Highway
#101 B

Pinellas Park
Ethan Allen Home Interiors
8901 U.S. Highway 19 North

Port Richey
Ethan Allen Home Interiors
9825 U.S. Highway 19

Stuart
Ethan Allen Home Interiors
1000 NW Federal Highway

Tampa
Ethan Allen Home Interiors
6200 North Dale Mabry
Highway

Ethan Allen Home Interiors
10015 Adamo Drive

Vero Beach
Ethan Allen Home Interiors
8505 20th Street
Route 60

West Palm Beach
Ethan Allen Home Interiors
2231 Palm Beach Lakes
Boulevard

GEORGIA

Alpharetta
Ethan Allen Home Interiors
6751 North Point Parkway

Atlanta
Ethan Allen Home Interiors
3221 Peachtree Road, NE

Augusta
Ethan Allen Home Interiors
3437 Wrightsboro Road

Buford
Ethan Allen Home Interiors
1885 Mall of Georgia Boulevard

Kennesaw
Ethan Allen Home Interiors
1005 Barrett Parkway

Smyrna
Ethan Allen Home Interiors
2205 Cobb Parkway

IDAHO

Boise
Ethan Allen Home Interiors
400 North Cole Road

ILLINOIS

Arlington Heights
Ethan Allen Home Interiors
1211 East Rand Road

Batavia
Ethan Allen Home Interiors
16 North Batavia Avenue

Bloomington
Ethan Allen Home Interiors
1344 East Empire

Chicago
Ethan Allen Home Interiors
1700 North Halsted

Countryside
Ethan Allen Home Interiors
6001 South LaGrange Road

Fairview Heights
Ethan Allen Home Interiors
455 Salem Place

Gurnee
Ethan Allen Home Interiors
3550 West Grand Avenue
at Route 41

Orland Park
Ethan Allen Home Interiors
15500 Harlem Avenue

Peoria
Ethan Allen Home Interiors
613 West Lake Street

Rockford
Ethan Allen Home Interiors
4720 East State Street

Skokie
Ethan Allen Home Interiors
10001 Skokie Boulevard

Wheaton
Ethan Allen Home Interiors
820 East Roosevelt Road

INDIANA

Evansville
Ethan Allen Home Interiors
7500 Eagle Crest Boulevard

Fort Wayne
Ethan Allen Home Interiors
1121 West Washington Center Road

Indianapolis
Ethan Allen Home Interiors
4905 East 82nd Street

Merrillville
Ethan Allen Home Interiors
8000 Broadway

Mishawaka
Ethan Allen Home Interiors
5225 North Main Street

IOWA

Cedar Rapids
Ethan Allen Home Interiors
1170 Twixt Town Road

Davenport
Ethan Allen Home Interiors
301 West Kimberly Road

Des Moines
Ethan Allen Home Interiors
7700 Hickman Road

KANSAS

Overland Park
Ethan Allen Home Interiors
6951 West 119th Street

Wichita
Ethan Allen Home Interiors
416 North Rock Road

KENTUCKY

Lexington
Ethan Allen Home Interiors
2191 Nicholasville Road

Louisville
Ethan Allen Home Interiors
9801 Linn Station Road

Paducah
Ethan Allen Home Interiors
114 North Third Street

LOUISIANA

Baton Rouge
Ethan Allen Home Interiors
8560 Florida Boulevard

Metairie
Ethan Allen Home Interiors
5300 Veterans Boulevard

Shreveport
Ethan Allen Home Interiors
8824 Youree Drive

MAINE

South Portland
Ethan Allen Home Interiors
160 Western Avenue

MARYLAND

Annapolis
Ethan Allen Home Interiors
2401 Solomons Island Road

Baltimore
Ethan Allen Home Interiors
6612 Baltimore National Pike

Frederick
Ethan Allen Home Interiors
5500 Buckeystown Pike

Rockville
Ethan Allen Home Interiors
1800 East Rockville Pike

Salisbury
Ethan Allen Home Interiors
306 West Main Street

Towson
Ethan Allen Home Interiors
8727 Loch Raven Boulevard

MASSACHUSETTS

Auburn
Ethan Allen Home Interiors
619 Southbridge Street
Route 12

Burlington
Ethan Allen Home Interiors
34 Cambridge Street

Hyannis
Ethan Allen Home Interiors
1520 Route 132

Natick
Ethan Allen Home Interiors
625 Worcester Road
Route 9

North Andover
Ethan Allen Home Interiors
419 Andover Street

Quincy
Ethan Allen Home Interiors
840 Willard Street

Saugus
Ethan Allen Home Interiors
636 Broadway
Route 1

Swansea
Ethan Allen Home Interiors
2241 GAR Highway

MICHIGAN

Ann Arbor
Ethan Allen Home Interiors
820 West Eisenhower
Cranbrook Village Parkway

Birmingham
Ethan Allen Home Interiors
275 North Old Woodward Avenue

Grand Blanc
Ethan Allen Home Interiors
10809 South Saginaw Road

Grand Rapids
Ethan Allen Home Interiors
3450 28th Street SE

Kalamazoo
Ethan Allen Home Interiors
6025 West Main Street

Lansing
Ethan Allen Home Interiors
8439 West Saginaw Road

Livonia
Ethan Allen Home Interiors
15700 Middlebelt Road

Novi
Ethan Allen Home Interiors
42845 Twelve Mile Road

Saginaw
Ethan Allen Home Interiors
5570 Bay Road

Sterling Heights
Ethan Allen Home Interiors
13725 Lakeside Circle

Traverse City
Ethan Allen Home Interiors
862 South Garfield Avenue

MINNESOTA

Eagan
Ethan Allen Home Interiors
1270 Promenade Place

Edina
Ethan Allen Home Interiors
7101 France Avenue South

Minnetonka
Ethan Allen Home Interiors
12320 Wayzata Boulevard

St. Paul
Ethan Allen Home Interiors
1111 Highway 36 East

MISSOURI

Chesterfield
Ethan Allen Home Interiors
15464 Olive Boulevard

Columbia
Ethan Allen Home Interiors
400 North Stadium Boulevard

Independence
Ethan Allen Home Interiors
18680 East 39th Street South

Kirkwood
Ethan Allen Home Interiors
10465 Manchester Road

Liberty
Ethan Allen Home Interiors
1 North Water Street
Southeast Corner of Square

Springfield
Ethan Allen Home Interiors
2825 South Glenstone
Battlefield Mall

MONTANA

Billings
Ethan Allen Home Interiors
3220 First Avenue North

NEBRASKA

Lincoln
Ethan Allen Home Interiors
70th and Van Dorn

Omaha
Ethan Allen Home Interiors
10720 Pacific Street

Ethan Allen Home Interiors
8001 West Dodge Road

NEVADA

Las Vegas
Ethan Allen Home Interiors
1540 South Rainbow
Boulevard

Reno
Ethan Allen Home Interiors
3445 Kietzke Lane

NEW HAMPSHIRE

Bedford
Ethan Allen Home Interiors
192 Route 101 West

Plaistow
Ethan Allen Home Interiors
Route 125

Portsmouth
Ethan Allen Home Interiors
755 Lafayette Road
Route 1

NEW JERSEY

Brick
Ethan Allen Home Interiors
110 Brick Plaza

Deptford
Ethan Allen Home Interiors
1692-F Clements Bridge Road
Locust Grove Plaza

East Brunswick
Ethan Allen Home Interiors
260 Route 18 North

Eatontown
Ethan Allen Home Interiors
164 Route 35 at South Street

Lawrenceville
Ethan Allen Home Interiors
2470 Brunswick Pike

Maple Shade
Ethan Allen Home Interiors
489 Route 38 West

Mays Landing
Ethan Allen Home Interiors
400 Consumer Square
2300 Wrangleboro Road

River Edge
Ethan Allen Home Interiors
Route 4 East and Main Street

Secaucus
Ethan Allen Home Interiors
850 Paterson Plank Road

Somerville
Ethan Allen Home Interiors
870 Route 22 East

Watchung
Ethan Allen Home Interiors
1541 Route 22

Wayne
Ethan Allen Home Interiors
475 Route 46 West

Whippany
Ethan Allen Home Interiors
245 Route 10

NEW MEXICO

Albuquerque
Ethan Allen Home Interiors
12521 Montgomery Boulevard
NE

NEW YORK

Amherst
Ethan Allen Home Interiors
3875 Sheridan Drive

Bay Shore
Ethan Allen Home Interiors
456 Montauk Highway

Clifton Park
Ethan Allen Home Interiors
15 Park Avenue, Shopper's
World

DeWitt
Ethan Allen Home Interiors
Dewey Avenue and East
Genesee

Forest Hills
Ethan Allen Home Interiors
112-33 Queens Boulevard

Garden City
Ethan Allen Home Interiors
750 Stewart Avenue

Hartsdale
Ethan Allen Home Interiors
152 South Central Avenue

Huntington Station
Ethan Allen Home Interiors
30 West Jericho Turnpike

Lake Grove
Ethan Allen Home Interiors
2758 Middle Country Road

Lynbrook
Ethan Allen Home Interiors
881 Sunrise Highway

Manhasset
Ethan Allen Home Interiors
1575 Northern Boulevard

Nanuet
Ethan Allen Home Interiors
300 East Route 59 and
Smith Street

Newburgh
Ethan Allen Home Interiors
94 North Plank Road

New York
Ethan Allen Home Interiors
1107 Third Avenue and
65th Street

Ethan Allen Home Interiors
192 Lexington Avenue and
32nd Street

Schenectady
Ethan Allen Home Interiors
2191 Central Avenue

Staten Island
Ethan Allen Home Interiors
2275 Richmond Avenue
Unit 21–23

Vestal
Ethan Allen Home Interiors
124 Sycamore Road

Victor
Ethan Allen Home Interiors
32 Eastview Mall Drive

NORTH CAROLINA

Asheville
Ethan Allen Home Interiors
Interstate 26 at Brevard Road

Cary
Ethan Allen Home Interiors
5717 Dillard Drive

Charlotte
Ethan Allen Home Interiors
7025 Smith Corner Boulevard

Pineville
Ethan Allen Home Interiors
11516 Carolina Place Parkway

Raleigh
Ethan Allen Home Interiors
7010 Glenwood Avenue

Wilmington
Ethan Allen Home Interiors
818 South College Road

NORTH DAKOTA

Fargo
Ethan Allen Home Interiors
1429 42nd Street SW

OHIO

Akron
Ethan Allen Home Interiors
55 Springside Drive

Centerville
Ethan Allen Home Interiors
821 Miamisburg at Centerville
Road

Chagrin Falls
Ethan Allen Home Interiors
8564 East Washington Street

Cincinnati
Ethan Allen Home Interiors
12151 Royal Point Drive

Kettering
Ethan Allen Home Interiors
1000 East Dorothy Lane

Mentor
Ethan Allen Home Interiors
7850 Mentor Avenue

North Olmsted
Ethan Allen Home Interiors
26127 Lorain Road

Reynoldsburg
Ethan Allen Home Interiors
6411 East Main Street

Springdale
Ethan Allen Home Interiors
11285 Princeton Pike

Toledo
Ethan Allen Home Interiors
6755 West Central Avenue

Worthington
Ethan Allen Home Interiors
6767 North High Street

Youngstown
Ethan Allen Home Interiors
8040 Market Street

OKLAHOMA

Oklahoma City
Ethan Allen Home Interiors
222 South Portland

Tulsa
Ethan Allen Home Interiors
6006 South Sheridan

OREGON

Beaverton
Ethan Allen Home Interiors
2800 NW Town Center Drive
Tanasbourne Town Center

Clackamas
Ethan Allen Home Interiors
12670 SE 82nd Avenue

Lake Oswego
Ethan Allen Home Interiors
15383 SW Bangy Road

Springfield
Ethan Allen Home Interiors
3150 Gateway Loop

PENNSYLVANIA

Allentown
Ethan Allen Home Interiors
5064 Hamilton Boulevard

Altoona
Ethan Allen Home Interiors
1 Sheraton Drive

Concordville
Ethan Allen Home Interiors
Routes 1 and 322

Dickson City
Ethan Allen Home Interiors
930 Viewmont Drive

East Petersburg
Ethan Allen Home Interiors
5139 Manheim Pike

Erie
Ethan Allen Home Interiors
7520 Peach Street

McMurray
Ethan Allen Home Interiors
2917 Washington Road

Monroeville
Ethan Allen Home Interiors
4685 William Penn Highway

Montgomeryville
Ethan Allen Home Interiors
668 Bethlehem Pike
Route 309

Paoli
Ethan Allen Home Interiors
1616 Lancaster Avenue

Trevose
Ethan Allen Home Interiors
4625 Street Road

Wexford
Ethan Allen Home Interiors
14010 Perry Highway

RHODE ISLAND

Warwick
Ethan Allen Home Interiors
1775 Bald Hill Road

SOUTH CAROLINA

Charleston
Ethan Allen Home Interiors
1821 A Sam Rittenberg
Boulevard

Columbia
Ethan Allen Home Interiors
101 Harbison Boulevard

Greenville
Ethan Allen Home Interiors
1184 North Pleasantburg Drive

SOUTH DAKOTA

Sioux Falls
Ethan Allen Home Interiors
2300 West 49th Street

TENNESSEE

Brentwood
Ethan Allen Home Interiors
1805 Mallory Lane

Cordova
Ethan Allen Home Interiors
1820 North Germantown
Parkway

Knoxville
Ethan Allen Home Interiors
10001 Kingston Pike

Nashville
Ethan Allen Home Interiors
2031 Richard Jones Road

TEXAS

Abilene
Ethan Allen Home Interiors
1380 South Clack at Hartford

Austin
Ethan Allen Home Interiors
2913 Anderson Lane

Beaumont
Ethan Allen Home Interiors
4755 East Texas Freeway

Corpus Christi
Ethan Allen Home Interiors
4325 South Padre Island Drive

Dallas
Ethan Allen Home Interiors
13920 North Dallas Parkway

Denton
Ethan Allen Home Interiors
200 West Oak Street

El Paso
Ethan Allen Home Interiors
5664 North Mesa Street

Friendswood
Ethan Allen Home Interiors
19240 Gulf Freeway

Houston
Ethan Allen Home Interiors
4081 R Westheimer Road

Ethan Allen Home Interiors
11431 Katy Freeway

Ethan Allen Home Interiors
16525 North Freeway

Hurst
Ethan Allen Home Interiors
633 NE Loop 820

Lewisville
Ethan Allen Home Interiors
2521 Stemmons Freeway

Mesquite
Ethan Allen Home Interiors
2330 Interstate 30

Odessa
Ethan Allen Home Interiors
2500 Andrews Highway

Richardson
Ethan Allen Home Interiors
305 South Central Expressway

San Antonio
Ethan Allen Home Interiors
2819 NW Loop 410

Stafford
Ethan Allen Home Interiors
12625 Southwest Freeway

Tyler
Ethan Allen Home Interiors
815 West Southwest Loop 323

UTAH

Salt Lake City
Ethan Allen Home Interiors
4545 South 900 East

VERMONT

Shelburne
Ethan Allen Home Interiors
2735 Shelburne Road

VIRGINIA

Fredericksburg
Ethan Allen Home Interiors
1480 Carl D. Silver Parkway

Glen Allen
Ethan Allen Home Interiors
10300 West Broad Street

Roanoke
Ethan Allen Home Interiors
4118 Electric Road

Springfield
Ethan Allen Home Interiors
6774 Springfield Mall

Vienna
Ethan Allen Home Interiors
8520-A Leesburg Pike

Virginia Beach
Ethan Allen Home Interiors
1554 Laskin Road, Unit 110
Hilltop East Shopping Center

Williamsburg
Ethan Allen Home Interiors
3032-1 Richmond Road

WASHINGTON

Lynnwood
Ethan Allen Home Interiors
4029 Alderwood Mall
Boulevard SW

Redmond
Ethan Allen Home Interiors
2209 NE Bellevue-Redmond
Road

Spokane
Ethan Allen Home Interiors
5511 East Third Avenue

Tukwila
Ethan Allen Home Interiors
17333 Southcenter Parkway

Yakima
Ethan Allen Home Interiors
411 West Yakima Avenue

WEST VIRGINIA

Huntington
Ethan Allen Home Interiors
5221 U.S. Route 60 East

Morgantown
Ethan Allen Home Interiors
122 Vista Del Rio Drive

WISCONSIN

Appleton
Ethan Allen Home Interiors
144 Mall Drive

Brookfield
Ethan Allen Home Interiors
14750 West Capitol Drive

Green Bay
Ethan Allen Home Interiors
2350 South Oneida Street

Greenfield
Ethan Allen Home Interiors
7740 West Layton Avenue

Madison
Ethan Allen Home Interiors
5302 Verona Road

Mequon
Ethan Allen Home Interiors
10900 North Port Washington Road

Wausau
Ethan Allen Home Interiors
2107 Robin Lane

INTERNATIONAL

BANGLADESH

Dhaka
Ethan Allen Home Interiors
House 3, Road 94
Gulshan 2

BRAZIL

São Paulo
Ethan Allen Home Interiors
Alameda Gabriel Monteiro
DaSilva, 949

Porte Alegre
Ethan Allen Home Interiors
Rua Eng. Alvaro
Pereira N 407, Apt. 601
Bairro Moinhos de Vento CEP

CANADA

Burlington
Ethan Allen Home Interiors
3225 Fairview Street

Calgary
Ethan Allen Home Interiors
Mayfair Place
6707 Elbow Drive SW

Coquitlam
Ethan Allen Home Interiors
1555 United Boulevard

Edmonton
Ethan Allen Home Interiors
17010 90th Avenue

Mississauga
Ethan Allen Home Interiors
2161 Dundas Street West

Pickering
Ethan Allen Home Interiors
1755 Pickering Parkway

Richmond
Ethan Allen Home Interiors
2633 Sweden Way

Thornhill
Ethan Allen Home Interiors
8134 Yonge Street

DOMINICAN REPUBLIC

Santo Domingo
Ethan Allen Home Interiors
Gustavo Mejia Ricart #124-A
Piantini

EGYPT

Cairo
Ethan Allen Home Interiors
2 Abdel Aziz Ei Hawary Street
Heliopolis

JAPAN

Chiba
Ethan Allen Home Interiors
IDC, 1-2-1 Tsudanuma
Narashino Shi

Osaka Shi
Ethan Allen Home Interiors
IDC, ATC Building, 8F
2-1-10 Nanko-Kita, Suminoe-Ku

Ethan Allen Home Interiors
1-17-28, Minami Horie,
Nishi-Ku

Saitama
Ethan Allen Home Interiors
1-9-7 Tyuou
Kasukabe Shi, Saitama

Tokyo
Ethan Allen Home Interiors
IDC TFT Building 4F
3-1 Ariake, Koto-Ku

KUWAIT

Kuwait City
Ethan Allen Home Interiors
Hassawi Street
Al Rai

MEXICO

Mexico City
Ethan Allen Home Interiors
Insurgentes Sur 1618

PHILIPPINES

Manila
Ethan Allen Home Interiors
Pioneer Street at Reliance Street
Mandaluyong City

SOUTH KOREA

Pusan
Ethan Allen Home Interiors
Dongwon Building
1078-16 Kwang-An 1 Dong,
Sooyong-Ku

Seoul
Ethan Allen Home Interiors
85-2 Chung Dam-Dong
Kangnam-Ku

Taegu
Ethan Allen Home Interiors
25-21 Daebong 1 Dong
Chung-Ku

TAIWAN

Kao-hsiung
Ethan Allen Home Interiors
No. 176 Ho-Tun Road 4F
Chen-Chin

Taipei
Ethan Allen Home Interiors
Design Center
C1010, No. 13, Lane 751
Kang-Ning Street Hsichin

Ethan Allen Home Interiors
Golden Sand Mega Store
23 Shin Hu 3rd Road, 2nd floor
Neihu District 114

UNITED ARAB EMIRATES

Dubai
Ethan Allen Home Interiors
Century Mall
Jumeirah Beach Road

Ethan Allen Home Interiors
Holiday Centre G/F
Sheikh Zayed Road